SCIENCE TECHNOLOGY ENGINEERING MATH

STEM QUEST

TOOLS, ROBOTICS, AND GADGETS GALORE

BARRON'S

First edition for the United States and
Canada published in 2018 by
Barron's Educational Series, Inc.

Text, design, and illustrations copyright
© Carlton Books Limited 2018,
an imprint of the Carlton Publishing Group,
20 Mortimer Street, London, WIT 3JW

All inquiries should be addressed to:
Barron's Educational Series, Inc.
250 Wireless Boulevard
Hauppauge, NY 11788
www.barronseduc.com

Executive editor: Selina Wood
Managing art editor: Dani Lurie
Design: Claire Barber
Illustrator: Annika Brandow
Picture research: Steve Behan
Production: Emma Smart
Editorial consultant: Jack Challoner

ISBN: 978-1-4380-1137-0

Library of Congress Control Number:
2017959665

Date of Manufacture: May 2018
Printed by Oriental Press, Jebel Ali,
Dubai, U.A.E.
9 8 7 6 5 4 3 2 1

AUTHOR
Nick Arnold

Nick Arnold is the author of many science
books for children, including a best-selling
series of yucky but entertaining science
facts. When he is not writing, Nick spends
his time giving talks to children in
bookstores, schools, and libraries.

STEM EDITORIAL CONSULTANT
Georgette Yakman

Georgette Yakman is the founding researcher and
creator of the integrative STEAM framework with
degrees in Integrated STEM Education, Technology,
and Fashion Design. She is the CEO of STEAM
Education and works in over 20 countries offering
educational professional development courses and
consulting as an international policy advisor.

ILLUSTRATOR
Kristyna Baczynski

Kristyna Baczynski is an Eisner-nominated comics
creator and illustrator. Her work has appeared
globally in a myriad of contexts, including magazines,
books, clothing, and curtains. If she were not an
illustrator, she would have been a biochemist,
so STEM is a subject close to her heart.

The publishers would like to thank the following sources for their
kind permission to reproduce the pictures in the book.

15. Universal History Archive/Universal Images Group/REX/
Shutterstock, 27. Getty Images, 34. Wellcome Library, London,
37. Granger/REX/Shutterstock, 47. Public Domain, 49. Library of
Congress, 51. Granger/REX/Shutterstock, 53. Joseph McKeown/
Picture Post/Getty Images, 55. Public Domain, 57. Granger/REX/
Shutterstock, 69. NASA

Every effort has been made to acknowledge correctly and contact
the source and/or copyright holder of each picture, and Carlton
Books apologizes for any unintentional errors or omissions, which will
be corrected in future editions of this book.

Adult supervision is recommended for all activities.

SCIENCE TECHNOLOGY ENGINEERING MATH

STEM QUEST

TOOLS, ROBOTICS, AND GADGETS GALORE

Nick Arnold

BARRON'S

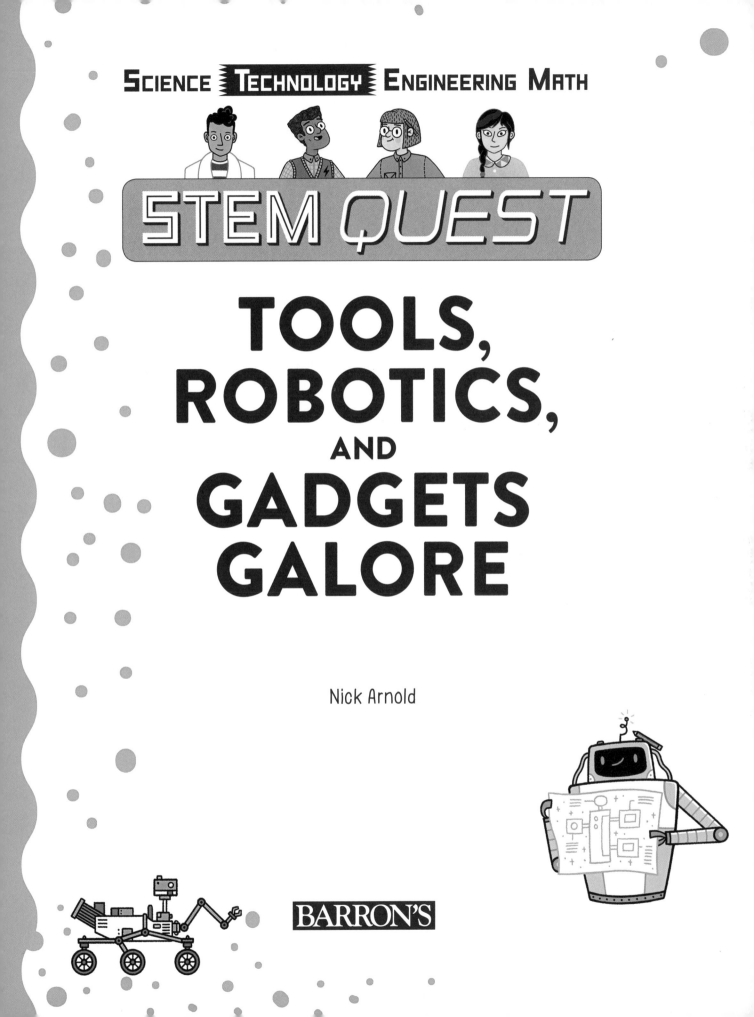

CONTENTS

Construction (including architecture)

Power & Energy

Agriculture & Biotechnology

Manufacturing

Information & Communication

Medical & Biomedical

Transportation

WELCOME TO STEM QUEST!

We're the **STEM Squad**, and we'd like to introduce you to the wonderful world of STEM: **Science, Technology, Engineering**, and **Math**. The **STEM Quest** series has a book on each of these fascinating subjects, and we are here to guide you through them. STEM learning gives you real-life examples and experiments to help you relate these subjects to the world around you. We hope you will discover that no matter who you are, you can be whatever you want to be: a scientist, an engineer, a technologist, or a mathematician. Let's take a closer look...

SCIENCE

In science you investigate the world around you.

Carlos and Ella

Super scientist **Carlos** is an expert on supernovas, gravity, and bacteria. **Ella** is Carlos's lab assistant. Carlos is planning a trip to the Amazon rain forest where Ella can collect, organize, and store data!

TECHNOLOGY

In technology you develop products and gadgets to improve our world.

Lewis and Violet

Top techy **Lewis** dreams of being on the first spaceship to Mars. Gadget genius **Violet** was built by Lewis from recycled trash.

ENGINEERING

In engineering you solve problems to create extraordinary structures and machines.

Olive and Clark

Olive is an incredible engineer who built her first skyscraper (out of dog biscuits) at the age of three. **Clark** was discovered by Olive on a trip to the pyramids of Giza.

MATH

In math you explore numbers, measurements, and shapes.

Sophie and Pierre

Math wizard **Sophie** impressed her class by working out the ratio of popcorn-lovers to doughnut-munchers. **Pierre** is Sophie's computer backup. His computer skills are helping to unlock the mystery of prime numbers.

TECHNOLOGY IS ABOUT DEVICES AND PROCESSES CREATED BY INVENTIVE PEOPLE.

Technology is a large range of useful products and ways of doing things. Some people think the pencil is the most important piece of technology invented. Almost every human old enough to write has used one to share his or her ideas. Throughout history, ideas have led to technologies that everyone uses, which are organized into eight categories. Learning about their history helps you discover the "magic" behind them and understand where they come from (science) and how they work (engineering, technology, and math). If you are good at it, you might be a problem-solver or a master of one of these amazing advancements!

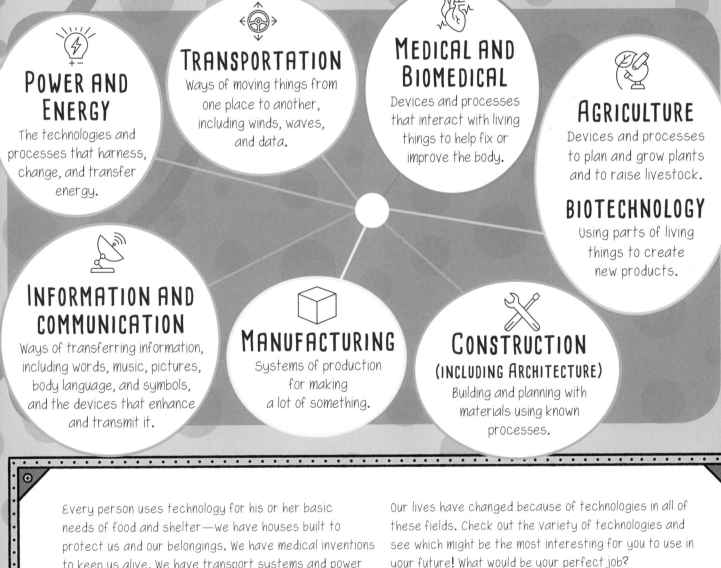

POWER AND ENERGY
The technologies and processes that harness, change, and transfer energy.

TRANSPORTATION
Ways of moving things from one place to another, including winds, waves, and data.

MEDICAL AND BIOMEDICAL
Devices and processes that interact with living things to help fix or improve the body.

AGRICULTURE
Devices and processes to plan and grow plants and to raise livestock.

BIOTECHNOLOGY
Using parts of living things to create new products.

INFORMATION AND COMMUNICATION
Ways of transferring information, including words, music, pictures, body language, and symbols, and the devices that enhance and transmit it.

MANUFACTURING
Systems of production for making a lot of something.

CONSTRUCTION (INCLUDING ARCHITECTURE)
Building and planning with materials using known processes.

Every person uses technology for his or her basic needs of food and shelter—we have houses built to protect us and our belongings. We have medical inventions to keep us alive. We have transport systems and power supplies, and we can transfer information to one another in many ways.

Our lives have changed because of technologies in all of these fields. Check out the variety of technologies and see which might be the most interesting for you to use in your future! What would be your perfect job?

Dream big, and good luck!

HANDY TOOLS

Technology began thousands of years ago when our ancestors first started to make tools for hunting, eating, building, and other basic jobs. One of the first hand tools was shaped like a wedge.

TRY THIS AT HOME

DRIVE A WEDGE

In this simple activity you're going to explore the power of the wedge shape!

YOU WILL NEED:

☑ Slices of hard cheese and apple

☑ A cutting board

☑ Four small stones (about 1–2 in/ 2–3 cm across) of different shapes —rounded, square-edged, and two that are wedge-shaped—narrow at one end and wide at the other. The wedge-shaped stones can be fat or short, thin or long (wash them first)

☑ A pencil and paper

1 Cut the cheese into "log" shapes, and place them on a cutting board.

2 Try cutting one of the cheese logs lengthwise with one of the stones. Do the same with three more cheese logs and three different stones.

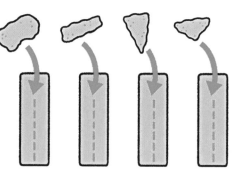

3 Write down or draw what you discover about how the different stones work when they cut the food.

4 Repeat steps 1 and 2 with the apple pieces.

WARNING! STONES MAY BE DIRTY. WASH BEFORE USE!

what's the BIG idea?

You will probably have found that the long, thin wedge-shaped stone cuts the cheese and apple pieces the most easily. Using a wedge not only increases the strength of the force but also changes the direction of the force. The force goes outward making it easier to break the pieces apart. The shallower the wedge angle the more the force is magnified—but the farther you have to push it into the pieces to break them.

input force

output force

a wedge shape

TRY THIS AT HOME

THE RIGHT TOOLS

Let's try out some hand tools you're likely to find in your home.

YOU WILL NEED:

- ✔ An adult helper
- ✔ Nails of different sizes
- ✔ Screws of different sizes
- ✔ Bolts of different sizes
- ✔ A piece of wood
- ✔ A screwdriver
- ✔ A hammer
- ✔ A wrench

nail

screw

bolt

piece of wood

screwdriver

wrench

hammer

1 Try making a simple face in the piece of wood using these tools. Figure out which ones you need to do the job. (Tip—use nails to start holes for screws!) Ask an adult to help you.

2 Have you figured out which tools are the easiest to use? Be careful not to bang your fingers with the hammer, too!

⚠ WARNING! SHARP AND HEAVY TOOLS!

what's the BIG idea?

Each tool is designed for a particular job. The hammer bashes the nail into the wood, whereas the screwdriver turns the screw into the wood. As for the wrench and bolt, they're not designed to go into the wood. All these tools require energy to do their jobs. You provide that energy from your muscles and your muscles obtain it from the food you eat.

SIMPLY EASIER

Over the centuries, inventors have strived to improve hand tools so that they are even easier to use. These more complex hand tools contain simple machines and mechanisms (moving parts that redirect a force). Let's explore!

what's the BIG idea?

Here are some of the simple mechanisms that form the basic parts of many machines.

HMM!

axle

wheel

The two parts of a wheel and axle are connected so that they always turn together. The rim of the wheel turns faster and farther than the axle—so if you turn the wheel, you can apply great force at the axle, but if you turn the axle, you can make the wheel turn much faster.

A **lever** is a rod balanced on a pivot called a **fulcrum**. With the fulcrum in the middle, the lever is balanced. The farther you move one end of the lever away, the less effort you need to exert force on the other side.

effort (force)

lever

fulcrum

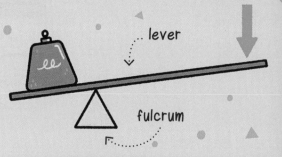

rack

pinion

Gears are toothed wheels that mesh together and change the speed, strength, or direction of turning forces in things like cars and bikes.

Rack and pinion mechanisms change a turning force to a sideways force.

HOW DOES IT WORK?

We see these simple mechanisms in everyday hand tools:

CAN OPENER

The handles (1) act like levers, concentrating the force of your hands onto the cutting edge. The gears direct the turning force of the handle (2) to the can.

handle (2)

rack and pinion

gears

handles (1)

HAND DRILL

A hand drill works like a wheel and axle. The motion of the drill handle concentrates a turning force on the drill bit.

drill handle

drill bit

MECHANICAL CORKSCREW

Pushing down the levers pulls the screw upward, raising the cork. A rack and pinion connects the levers to the screw so the cork can move up and down.

handle

lever

screw

PUZZLE ZONE

MIXED-UP EGGBEATER

crown wheel

shaft

gears

handle

beaters

gears

Which of these mechanisms are found in this eggbeater?

A) LEVER

B) WHEEL AND AXLE

C) GEARS

CAN YOU GUESS?

HOW DOES IT WORK?

The handle, shaft, and crown wheel of the eggbeater act like a wheel and axle, concentrating the turning force of the handle onto the crown wheel. The crown wheel and gears at the end of the beater rods redirect the turning force to the beaters and boost the beaters' speed. The mechanism you won't find in the eggbeater is a lever (A).

IN FACT...
EARLY EGGBEATERS

Nowadays you're likely to come across an eggbeater as part of an electric mixer. But did you know the first eggbeaters were bundles of apple twigs? They gave an apple flavor to cooking.

LET'S GET COOKING!

Our clever ancestors first learned about the power of heat when they discovered how to control fire for cooking and keeping warm. Read on for the full, fiery facts!

what's the BIG idea?

FIRE!

Fire is the result of a **chemical reaction** known as **combustion**. The **atoms** (particles) from **hydrogen** and **carbon** in the fuel (such as wood) combine with **oxygen** atoms from the air. This reaction produces **carbon dioxide** and water—as well as heat and light.

oxygen in the air

= carbon dioxide + water + heat + light

hydrogen and carbon in wood

TRY THIS AT HOME

IT'S TOAST!

YOU WILL NEED:

- ✔ An adult helper
- ✔ An oven or toaster oven
- ✔ A slice of bread

1 Get an adult to help you turn on the oven and heat it to about 350°F (177°C).

2 Place a slice of bread directly onto the rack and toast one side of the bread for 5—7 minutes.

3 Now compare the color, smell, and taste of the two sides of the bread.

WHAT'S GOING ON?

When you toast bread in an oven or in a toaster, you cause a chemical reaction at the surface of the bread. Chemicals react when you bake bread—the **proteins** in the yeast give the bread its smell and they "feed" off the sugars that add to the browning.

WARNING! HOT!

MAKE A SOLAR OVEN

Did you know that you can use **solar** (the sun's) energy to cook food? Try this out on a warm, summer day!

YOU WILL NEED:

- ✔ An adult helper
- ✔ A thick pizza delivery box
- ✔ Black paint (matte) and paintbrush or black paper
- ✔ Aluminum foil
- ✔ Newspaper
- ✔ A ruler
- ✔ A raw egg to fry
- ✔ A plate
- ✔ Plastic wrap

WARNING! BEWARE, HEAT!

1 Paint the bottom of the pizza box black or cover it with black paper. Line the inside lid of the box with foil.

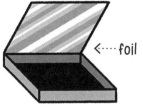
foil

2 Roll up the newspaper into four columns, and place them along the four sides of the base.

newspaper

3 Use a ruler to keep the top of the box open.

ruler

4 Crack the egg onto a plate. Put the plate on the base of the box. Cover the plate and base of the box with plastic wrap.

plastic wrap

5 Place the box so that the sun shines on the inside. It works best between the hours of 12 P.M. and 3 P.M.—you may find it takes a while. Angle the lid or prop up the box with a ruler or other object to reflect the most light onto the egg. Leave your egg in the sun to cook. You should be able to watch the clear part of the egg turn white and the yellow yolk get hard. Do not eat liquid egg whites!

HOW DOES IT WORK?

The sun's rays become trapped in the pizza box and heat it up. The warm rays shine onto the foil and are reflected onto the egg. The plastic wrap helps to trap the warm air. The black paper or paint absorbs the heat, keeping the base of the box warm. What happens to the egg? The egg contains particles called **molecules** (atoms joined together) that are rolled up in tiny ball-like structures. The heat unravels them and reshapes them, turning the egg from liquid to solid as it cooks.

EGG-WHITE MOLECULES

before heating   after heating

IN FACT...

ANCIENT COOKING

- Some of the first ovens were fire pits dug in Europe 29,000 years ago. They were used to cook mammoth meat.

- The ancient Greeks used front-loaded bread ovens over 3,000 years ago.

- Metal stoves weren't common until the 1800s.

CERAMICS

A good techie knows that heat can harden or melt all sorts of materials. One such material that heat hardens is ceramics. Ceramics can become rigid and waterproof by heating clay (fine particles of rock or earth) in an oven called a kiln. Let's check them out.

ceramic pot

what's the BIG idea?

NATURAL OR PROCESSED?

Natural clay is soft. When you heat it, water **evaporates** from it, and new bonds form between the clay particles in a process that produces a stronger, harder material.

kiln

TRY THIS AT HOME

MAKE SALTY CLAY

OK, so this "clay" isn't the real deal—but you'll get a feel for how clay can be molded into shapes. The only thing you can't do is EAT it!

YOU WILL NEED:

- ✔ An adult helper
- ✔ 1 cup of water
- ✔ A measuring cup
- ✔ 1 cup of salt
- ✔ 2 cups of flour
- ✔ A pot
- ✔ A wooden spoon
- ✔ A stove or hot plate and oven/microwave

1 With adult help, gently heat 1 cup of water (no need to boil). Slowly stir in 1 cup of salt, and continue stirring until the salt dissolves.

salt

flour

2 Little by little, add 2 cups of flour, stirring all the while. Continue stirring to make a smooth paste. Add a little more water or flour to get a clay consistency. Heat the mixture until it thickens.

1 HR

3 Allow the mixture to cool, knead it to make it smooth, then shape it into something amazing. Heat the oven to 200°F (90°C) and bake your creation for about an hour. Smaller items can be placed in a microwave for 10-15 second bursts until they dry.

WARNING! BEWARE, HEAT!

HOW DOES IT WORK?

As your salt dough clay dries, particles in the flour become bonded together, and the salt dough hardens.

WHAT'S GOING ON?

Glass is another ceramic material. It's made from a substance called silicon dioxide, which is found in sand. It's heated until runny and then shaped and cooled quickly. The result is a transparent material. Glass is not a true solid—the molecules that form it are arranged in no clear order, a bit like those of a liquid.

GLASS MOLECULE

oxygen atom

silicon atom

Glass can sometimes be blown into shape because of its runny, sticky consistency when hot. It gradually hardens into a firm shape as it loses heat.

WHO WAS WEDGWOOD?

Josiah Wedgwood (1730–1795) was a British potter who opened pottery factories and made ornamental pots—some of his most famous being distinctive blue and white. He invented the pyrometer, an instrument for measuring the temperature of kilns.

AMAZING METALS

From gold to aluminum and copper to silver, metals are everywhere. Metals are natural materials extracted from the ground. Most are solid, with a gray or silver appearance, and are vital materials for techies.

what's the BIG idea?

HARDY MATERIAL

Most metals are tough, hard, and strong. Many can be drawn into wires or beaten into panels. These qualities make metals useful materials for construction and for creating tools and machines, such as computers, cars, and planes.

Many metals are found in the earth in rocks called **ores**. People have discovered different ways to extract them. In one process called smelting, ore is heated to a high temperature until it melts, and the molten metal is separated out.

metal ore

HOW DOES A BLAST FURNACE WORK?

The metal iron is extracted from iron ore in a huge heated container called a blast furnace. Limestone (rock) and coke (a fuel made from coal) are added to help the chemical reaction that separates the pure iron from the rest of the ore.

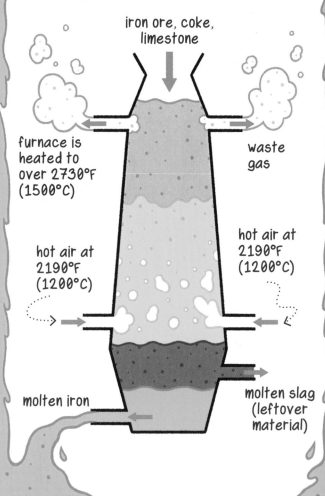

iron ore, coke, limestone

furnace is heated to over 2730°F (1500°C)

waste gas

hot air at 2190°F (1200°C)

hot air at 2190°F (1200°C)

molten iron

molten slag (leftover material)

METAL MATTERS

paper clip

Let's put some metals to the test to see what they can do.

1 Start making a simple chart by writing the name of each of your metals at the top of three columns.

YOU WILL NEED:

- ✔ A pencil
- ✔ Paper
- ✔ A hard, 90° corner, such as the edge of a tabletop
- ✔ Three types of metal wire—for instance, copper, aluminum, and stainless steel (you can use a paper clip for stainless steel)

WARNING! WATCH THE SHARP EDGE OF THE TABLE!

2 Open the paper clip into an "S" shape.

3 Place a piece of the paperclip on the hard, 90° edge, and bend it until it is folded down against the corner. Then fold it out flat again. Count this as one full bend. Try bending it a few times.

4 Do this with each wire, and count each bend until the wire breaks. This is the metal's "elasticity" or its ability to bend and unbend and still be the same shape. Write your results on the chart.

5 Which wires were stronger? Why do you think they were stronger? Were they thicker? You could try this experiment again with wires that are all the same thickness and length.

HOW DOES IT WORK?

Some wires are softer than others and bend easily. Aluminum and gold are examples of softer metals. Others are brittle and break when bent, but they are stronger or more useful in other ways. Steel is an alloy: a mixture made of at least one metal. Steel is mostly iron and carbon and is strong, but it can also be stretched. It is used to make lots of things, including bridges and buildings.

YANK!

IN FACT...

CLEVER COMPOSITES

There are many things that seem to be metal but have other things mixed in them to make them suited to a particular use. Mixed metals are alloys, but adding in a ceramic or polymer will make the mixture a composite. For instance, a tennis racket may be made out of a mix of materials known for their strength and lightness. Composites are mostly synthetic (made by humans), though a few exist in the natural world.

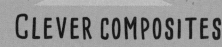

FANTASTIC PLASTIC

You don't have to look very far before you spot something made of plastic. It's in many things from food packaging to toys and phones. Techies use plastic because it's strong and light and can be molded into many shapes.

what's the BIG idea?

Most plastics are synthetic. Many are made from molecules found in oil, coal, and gas.

Plastics are a type of polymer. Polymers are long chains of molecules containing carbon, hydrogen, and sometimes other types of atoms. The molecule chains are created by chemical reactions.

TRY THIS AT HOME

MAKE YOUR OWN PLASTIC

Now's your chance to make you own rubbery plastic!

YOU WILL NEED:

- ✔ An adult helper
- ✔ Whole milk (not skim)
- ✔ A measuring cup
- ✔ Vinegar
- ✔ A teaspoon
- ✔ A pot
- ✔ A bowl
- ✔ A fine strainer
- ✔ A stove or hot plate
- ✔ A wooden spoon

1 Ask an adult to help you heat 5 fl oz (150 ml) of milk until it simmers.

vinegar

2 Add 4 teaspoons of vinegar.

3 Stir until clumps form, and then remove the pot from the heat.

4 Pour the mixture through the strainer into the bowl.

5 Carefully pour off the remaining liquid, and squish together the solids to make a shape.

HOW DOES IT WORK?

Congratulations! You've made a rubbery plastic! Like all plastics, it's made up of long, stringy molecules. In this case, the molecules are a type of protein called **casein**. The **acid** in the vinegar separates the protein and the fat in the milk. The protein forms the blobs.

fat

protein

TESTING TIME!

Tests—ugh! Fortunately this time it's YOU doing the testing!

YOU WILL NEED:

- ✔ An adult helper
- ✔ A small plastic object (bottle cap)
- ✔ A small metal object of the same size (key)
- ✔ A magnet
- ✔ Tape
- ✔ A hammer
- ✔ A mug
- ✔ A kettle and a stove or hot plate (hot water)

1 Try to pick up each of the objects with the magnet.

2 Drop them from an equal height onto a hard floor.

3 Ask an adult to help you pour some hot water from a kettle into a mug. Tape each item to the side of the mug for five minutes, then hold them to your skin.

4 Go outside, place them on the ground, and hit each one equally hard with the hammer.

! WARNING! HEAVY HAMMER AND HOT WATER!

WHAT'S GOING ON?

Your tests highlight some of the differences between metals and plastics. Metals are usually hard and some are magnetic, and they also conduct (let heat through easily). Plastics aren't magnetic and they don't let heat through so easily. Plastics are often bouncy and softer than metals. Can you think of any other tests you might try?

PUZZLE ZONE

Which materials would you use for...

1. A monster's cage?

2. A ball for kids to play with?

3. A high-tech base in the Antarctic?

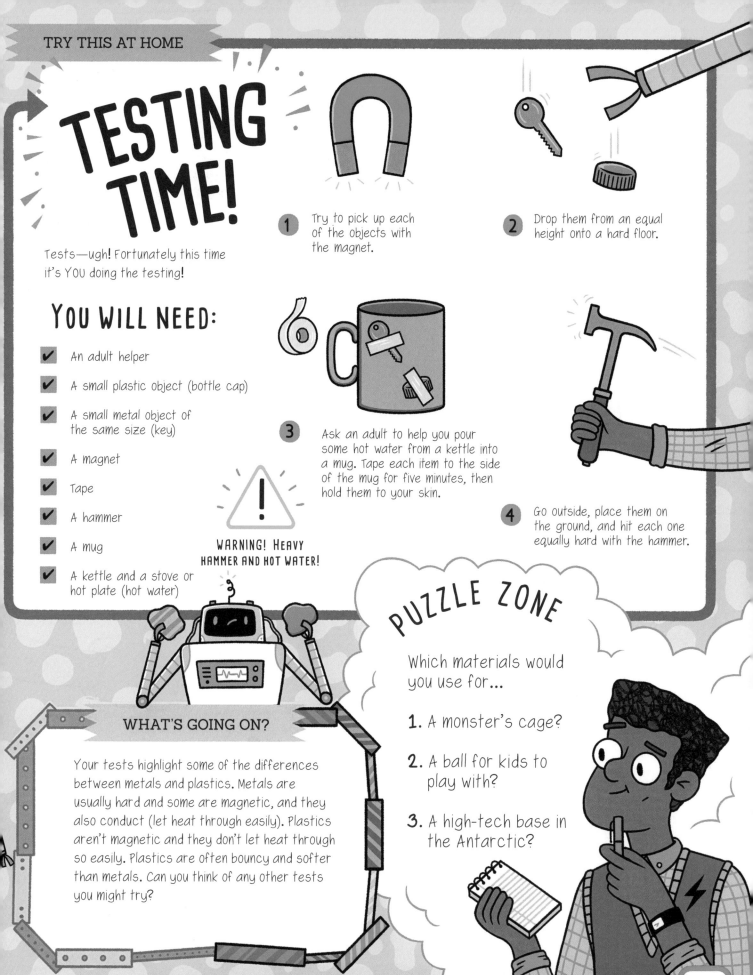

ANSWERS ARE AT THE BACK OF THE BOOK

TERRIFIC TEXTILES

From fabulous fashions to crazy carpets, our lives are full of fabrics, cloth, and textiles. But here's the question—what makes textiles, textiles? Let's find out!

→ what's the **BIG** idea?

MAKING TEXTILES

Long, thin strands, known as fibers, are spun into yarns (or threads). The fibers can be natural like wool (from sheep), cotton (from cotton plants), or silk (from silkworms.) They can also be synthetic (made by humans) like **polyester** and **nylon**. Yarns are then woven into fabrics or wools.

silkworm

cotton plant

TRY THIS AT HOME

TEXTILE TESTER

YOU WILL NEED:

✔ Old items made from natural fibers, such as wool and cotton

✔ Old items made from synthetic fibers, such as polyester or nylon

✔ Ice cubes

✔ A pen and paper

⚠️ **WARNING! DON'T TOUCH ICE WITH BARE HANDS— IT CAN BURN!**

1 Wrap your hand in each material, and then pick up some ice cubes. Which textile keeps your hand warm the longest? Write down your results.

BRRR!

YANK!

SPLASH!

2 Place each textile in a sink and pour a glass of water over it. Which textile soaks up the most water? Write down your results.

3 Stretch each textile with equal force. Which one stretches the most, and which one loses its shape? Write down your results.

HOW DOES IT WORK?

What did you discover about natural and synthetic fibers? Wool, with its loose weave, traps air and is warm to wear. Nylon, with its tight weave, is more resistant to water. Cotton absorbs a lot of water and is cool to wear.

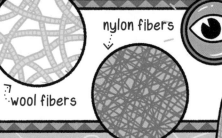

nylon fibers

wool fibers

TRY THIS AT HOME

WOVEN WONDERS

Let's experiment with weaving technology.

YOU WILL NEED:

- ✔ A piece of stiff cardboard
- ✔ Scissors
- ✔ Yarn
- ✔ Old pieces of fabric (ideally with different colors or patterns)
- ✔ A pencil
- ✔ Fabric glue
- ✔ A ruler with metric and imperial measurements

lines

yarn

1 Mark an even number of lines at opposite ends of the cardboard. The lines should be 1.5 cm apart. Each line should be opposite a line at the other end.

2 Cut the lines to make slits. Stretch some yarn from the slit in a top corner to the slit in the opposite bottom corner. You should leave at least 10 cm of spare yarn at the top. Take the yarn behind the cardboard to the next slit along at the bottom, and stretch the yarn to the opposite slit at the top.

3 Repeat step 2 going from end to end of the cardboard until all the slits have been used.

4 Leave enough yarn to tie off the two ends of yarn at the back of the cardboard.

5 Cut strips of fabric about 1 cm wide and 2 cm longer than the width of the cardboard.

6 Turn the cardboard over, and weave the fabric strips in and out of the yarn. Glue the fabric ends to the back of the cardboard.

glue

HOW DOES IT WORK?

Your creation is a woven work of art! The cardboard is a simple loom, a device that is used for weaving cloth.

MAKE YOUR MARK

Technology is more than gadgets and gigabytes—it's about a spectrum of colors and ink for dying and printing, too. Go on techies—express yourselves!

COLORS TO DYE FOR!

Early people first used natural **dyes** (made from animals and plants) to create cave art. But people soon learned to dye woven cloth. These days a lot of dyes are synthetic.

YOU WILL NEED:

- ✔ An adult helper
- ✔ A white cotton T-shirt
- ✔ Rubber bands
- ✔ Red cabbage
- ✔ White vinegar
- ✔ Rubber gloves
- ✔ Old clothes
- ✔ A large spoon
- ✔ A fine strainer
- ✔ Water
- ✔ A pot
- ✔ 2 tablespoons of salt
- ✔ A stove or hot plate

1 Dress in your old clothes and wear rubber gloves —this is going to get messy!

rubber bands

2 Accordion fold your T-shirt and wrap it with rubber bands, as shown above.

vinegar

3 Mix ½ gallon (2 liters) of water with 17 fl oz (500 ml) of vinegar in a pot. Ask an adult to heat the mixture until it begins to boil. Add the T-shirt, and simmer for one hour.

⚠️ **WARNING! BEWARE HEAT AND MESS! HEAT DRY T-SHIRT BEFORE WASHING WITH OTHER CLOTHES**

red cabbage
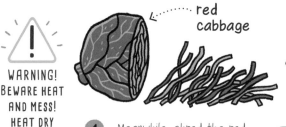

4 Meanwhile, shred the red cabbage. Cover it in water, and ask an adult to simmer it for at least one hour. This is your dye.

5 Dunk the T-shirt in cold water, then squeeze the water out.

6 When the dye is ready, strain out the cabbage, and dunk the T-shirt in the dye. Top off with hot water if required, and stir well.

7 When the T-shirt is a deep purple color you can remove it and rinse it with cold water until the water runs clear. Leave it in salted water to set the dye.

SPLASH!

8 Remove the rubber bands, and hang your T-shirt out to dry. You may want to tumble dry it so that the dye is less likely to leak in future washes. Wash it separately until no more dye leaks from it.

HOW DOES IT WORK?

Congratulations, you have a streaky, purple shirt! So how does the dye stick to the T-shirt fabric? Red cabbage contains a **pigment** that is a strong natural dye. A chemical reaction takes place in which molecules in the dye attach to the molecules in the fabric. A similar process takes place when you spill food and stain your clothes. Adding vinegar turns the pigment a purplish red.

TRY THIS AT HOME

GET INTO PRINT

Now let's take a closer look at ink and the wonders of printing.

YOU WILL NEED:

- ✔ Household objects, such as a screw, a nut, an eraser, a brick, half of a potato, etc.
- ✔ Six colors of poster paints
- ✔ Paper
- ✔ A pen

1 With six different objects and six different-colored paints, make up an alphabet of 24 letters based on colors and shapes. For example, a red cross-headed screw could be an "A." Write down what your alphabet will be.

red cross-headed screw = A

blue nut = B

green brick = C

yellow potato = D

orange eraser = E

purple bottle top = F

2 Print your name using your newly invented alphabet. You'll need to dip the item in the relevant color (make sure there's not too much paint on it) and press it onto the paper.

HOW DOES IT WORK?

You're printing! Early printers worked in much the same way. They developed racks to put metal letters on and machines to press them down on the paper. The letters had to be placed backward so they would end up facing the correct way once printed.

PAPER POWER!

You see and use it so often, you hardly notice it! But we'd be lost without it. Techies, let's test out the power of paper!

1. Trees are felled (cut down)

2. Logs are cut into chips

3. Water is added to wood chips and pulped

WHAT'S GOING ON?

HOW IS PAPER MADE?

It's strange to think that paper is made from mighty trees. How is that possible? Here's how...

4. Wood pulp is dried and pressed ...

5. ... and cut into paper sheets

TRY THIS AT HOME

WACKY WATER TEST

How can we make water "walk?" Don't be baffled, techies—all will be revealed!

YOU WILL NEED:

- ✔ Blue food coloring
- ✔ Yellow food coloring
- ✔ Paper towels and tissue paper
- ✔ Three glasses
- ✔ Two wooden spoons

1 Fill two glasses two-thirds full of water. Stir in enough blue food coloring into one glass to make a strong blue. Do the same for the yellow food coloring in the second glass.

2 Fold a paper towel in half lengthwise, and then fold it again lengthwise. Do the same for the second paper towel.

3 Put the third empty glass in the middle of the first two, and set up the experiment as shown. Watch what happens. Afterward, why not repeat the activity with tissue paper, too?

blue coloring   yellow coloring

paper towel

blue   yellow

HOW DOES IT WORK?

The water flows up both paper towels, taking the color with it. Water flows into the middle glass and the colors mix to make green! So how can water flow upward? Paper is made of microscopic natural fibers called cellulose. This comes from paper's original source, trees. Cellulose particles attract water, and because water molecules are drawn to each other, more water soaks into the paper towel. Paper towels and tissue paper have big air spaces so they can soak up a lot of water.

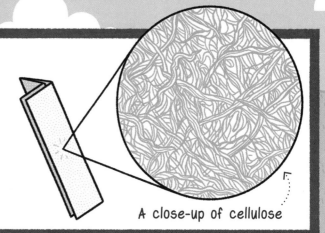

A close-up of cellulose

TRY THIS AT HOME

PAPER FORTUNE TELLER

YOU WILL NEED:

- ✔ A piece of rectangular white paper
- ✔ Scissors
- ✔ Colored pencils

1 Turn the rectangular paper into a square by folding one corner over to the opposite side. Cut off the small rectangle to leave a square.

2 Fold all four corners into the middle of the paper.

3 Then turn the paper over and fold all four corners into the middle again.

4 Flip the paper over again so that the squares are facing up. Color each square a different color.

5 Turn it over so that the triangles are facing up. Number each triangle 1–8.

write numbers

6 Open up the triangles and write a fortune under each number. It could be "You will meet interesting people" or "You will travel to great places" or anything you like!

7 Flip it over so the squares are facing up. Fold it in half so that you can get your first finger and thumb on each hand into the four corners.

8 Get a friend to pick one of the colors. Spell out the color, by moving the fortune teller from back to front and from side to side, the number of letters in the word (red has 3 letters, so move it 3 times).

9 Ask your friend to choose a number. Move the fortune teller that number of times. Then ask your friend to choose another number. Open up the fortune teller and read out the fortune under the number to your friend!

HOW DOES IT WORK?

It may look flimsy but paper is useful because it can be folded into different shapes. Some papers are stronger than others. They may have more fibers or the fibers may be longer and more tangled. Or the paper may be treated with a strengthening substance, such as **resin**.

HMM!

GO WITH THE FLOW

Water acts like it has a mind of its own—it leaks, it drips, and it tends to flow wherever it wants! So, techies, we need a plan. How do we control it?

HOW DO WE MOVE AND CONTAIN WATER?

People have always tried to control the flow of liquids. In ancient Egypt, over two thousand years ago, people used ditches, **shadoofs**, and Archimedes screws to channel water for crops. In ancient China, people built canal gates. Today, **engines** and central heating systems all rely on **pumps** to move liquids.

shadoof

Archimedes screw

canal gates

GET PUMPING!

We use pumps every day. Let's look at how they work.

YOU WILL NEED:

✔ A pump from a liquid soap dispenser
✔ Two glasses of water

1. Wash the pump thoroughly to get rid of the soap.

2. Place the lower tube in a glass of water. Hold the other glass under the dispenser and push the pump handle repeatedly.

SPLASH!

water

HOW DOES IT WORK?

When you push down the pump...

1. The **piston** is pressed down into a chamber.

2. Water in the chamber is forced up the hollow center of the piston and out of the dispenser. The chamber empties.

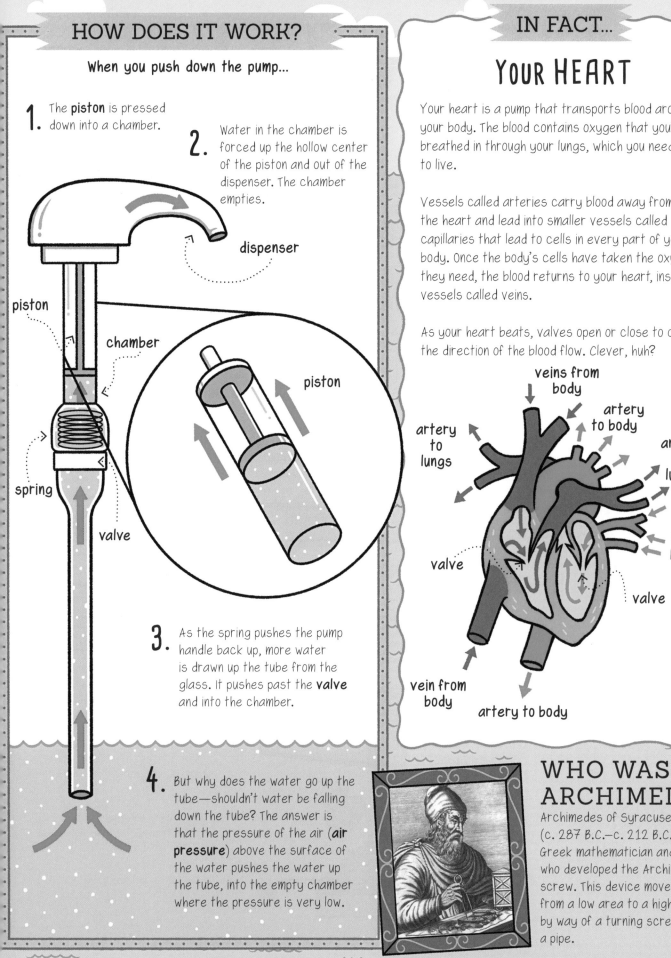

dispenser

piston

chamber

piston

spring

valve

3. As the spring pushes the pump handle back up, more water is drawn up the tube from the glass. It pushes past the **valve** and into the chamber.

4. But why does the water go up the tube—shouldn't water be falling down the tube? The answer is that the pressure of the air (**air pressure**) above the surface of the water pushes the water up the tube, into the empty chamber where the pressure is very low.

YOUR HEART

Your heart is a pump that transports blood around your body. The blood contains oxygen that you've breathed in through your lungs, which you need to live.

Vessels called arteries carry blood away from the heart and lead into smaller vessels called capillaries that lead to cells in every part of your body. Once the body's cells have taken the oxygen they need, the blood returns to your heart, inside vessels called veins.

As your heart beats, valves open or close to control the direction of the blood flow. Clever, huh?

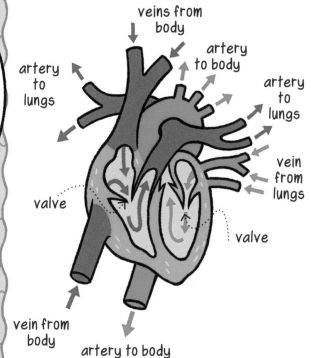

veins from body

artery to body

artery to lungs

artery to lungs

vein from lungs

valve

valve

vein from body

artery to body

WHO WAS ARCHIMEDES?

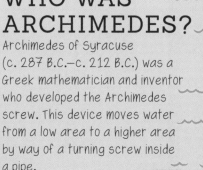

Archimedes of Syracuse (c. 287 B.C.–c. 212 B.C.) was a Greek mathematician and inventor who developed the Archimedes screw. This device moves water from a low area to a higher area by way of a turning screw inside a pipe.

MUSCLES ON THE MOVE

Give techies heavy cargo to transport, and what will they do? Easy—they will figure out a way to make the effort easier. Could you?

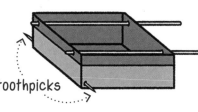

TRY THIS AT HOME

BUILD A WHEELBARROW

A wheelbarrow sounds basic, but there's a lot of techie science behind it. Let's discover the wonder of the wheelbarrow.

YOU WILL NEED:

- ✔ An adult helper
- ✔ A small, open cardboard box—roughly 4 x 4 in (10 x 10 cm) big
- ✔ Weights (can be household objects)
- ✔ Two wooden skewers or straws (they need to be long enough to go through the box)
- ✔ Two toothpicks
- ✔ Packing tape
- ✔ Scissors
- ✔ Corrugated cardboard
- ✔ A small, circular object, like a bottle top

1 Place the weight in the box, and try pulling or pushing it forward across the ground.

2 Wrap packing tape around the top of the sides of the box, and push two of the skewers through at either side. Cut off the sharp ends of the skewers.

skewer

packing tape

skewer

3 Push a toothpick into the side of the front of the box, a little way up from the bottom. Do the same in the exact spot on the opposite side of the box. Tape the sticks together where they meet.

toothpicks

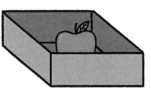

corrugated cardboard

4 Trace your circular object onto the corrugated cardboard twice, and cut the circles out. These are your wheels. Remember that the distance from the middle to the edge of each wheel will need to be the same as the distance from the toothpick on your box to the floor when you attach the wheels. Push the toothpicks through the middle of your wheels.

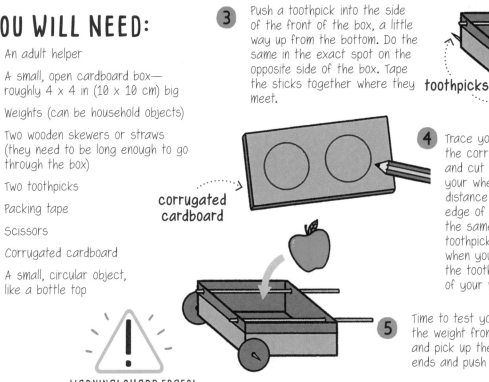

5 Time to test your wheelbarrow. Put the weight from step 1 into the box, and pick up the two longer skewer ends and push the wheelbarrow along.

⚠ WARNING! SHARP EDGES!

28

HOW DOES IT WORK?

A wheelbarrow has two levers with a fulcrum where the axle meets the wheels (see p. 10). When you lift the handles you move them a distance, resulting in a stronger force to lift the load end. It's easier to push the load along with wheels rather than without, as there's less friction—the force that resists the movement of two surfaces rubbing against each other. However, some friction is needed for the wheels to move—you'll probably find it easier to push your wheelbarrow along a rough surface than on a smooth surface.

lever

lever

cargo

fulcrum

axle

HOW DO BICYCLES WORK?

Like the wheelbarrow, a bike combines wheels and axles with levers to make moving easier. But bikes also have pedals to produce force and gears to control the force. The gears can change the speed and force with which the wheels turn.

The gears on a bike are connected to the pedals with a chain. You can change between smaller and bigger gears to help you keep a steady speed, whether you ride uphill or downhill.

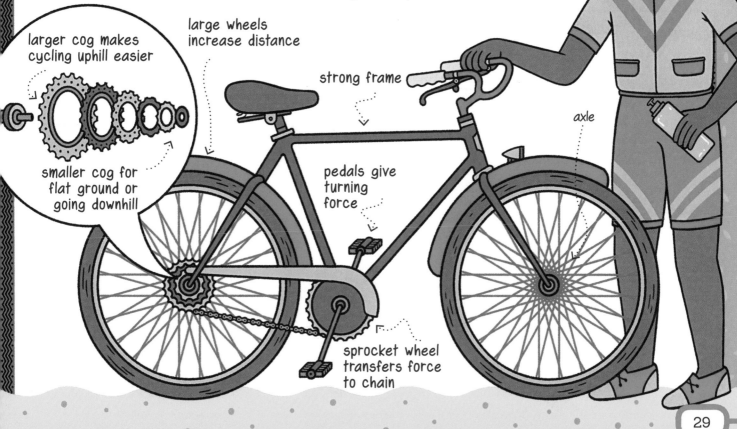

larger cog makes cycling uphill easier

smaller cog for flat ground or going downhill

large wheels increase distance

strong frame

axle

pedals give turning force

sprocket wheel transfers force to chain

29

POWERING AHEAD

If you're a techie, you may be looking for something a little faster than a bicycle. You aren't just happy with fast—you want VERY fast. So that means adding an engine to your wheels. Ready for a spin?

→ what's the **BIG** idea?

HOW DO POWERED VEHICLES WORK?

If you build a powered vehicle, you need to build a **motor** that is powerful enough to move your vehicle and light enough not to slow it down. It would need to carry its own fuel, which can't be too heavy either. It MUST be safe!

TRAINS OR CARS? Let's compare them.

COMPARE...	TRAINS	CARS
WHEELS	Lots!	Usually four
TRAVELS ON	Rails. Friction between the train wheels and the rails helps to keep the train moving and under control.	Roads mostly. Like the wheels on a train, the friction between the car tires and the road helps to keep the car moving.
POWER	Trains run on diesel or **steam**, or electric power from rails or overhead lines.	Cars run on petrol, ethanol, or diesel fuel. Sometimes they have **electric motors**.
STEERING	Trains have no steering—the wheels follow the shape of the track, and trains are run from a control center.	Cars have full steering—a complex steering system.
SLOPES	Trains can't manage steep slopes.	Some cars can manage slopes much steeper than the 35° seen here.
LOADS	Trains can carry thousands of pounds or hundreds of tons. One ton is about the weight of a very small car.	A second engine can occasionally be added to a car to boost power. Few cars can carry more than about 800 lbs (400 kg).

STEAM CARS

Some early cars were powered by engines run by steam. They were not easy to run—they needed lots of water and they burned solid fuel, such as coal. Steam engines were fine for big, heavy vehicles like trains, but they were not so good for cars.

TRY THIS AT HOME

DRIVING PRACTICE

Get ready to drive a car without even touching it—as if by magic!

YOU WILL NEED:

- ✔ A small toy car
- ✔ Two powerful bar magnets
- ✔ Masking tape
- ✔ Smooth, plastic tape

magnet ······>

masking tape

1 Tape one magnet to your toy car roof.

2 Make a track by sticking masking tape to the floor. Why not add a few obstacles, too?

3 Use the second magnet to pull or push your car around your track. Hold the north or south pole of the magnet behind the same pole of the magnet on the car. The magnets should repel each other, and you can push the car along. Now try driving the car on smooth, plastic tape.

HOW DOES IT WORK?

Unlike a real car, your toy car gets its power from the magnetic force between the two magnets. But like a real car, there needs to be some friction between your car wheels and the driving surface in order for the car wheels to turn. The masking tape is rougher than the plastic tape, so there's more friction. Try driving your car on other surfaces to discover which ones let your car move the easiest.

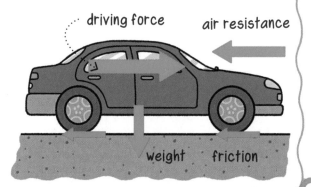

driving force   air resistance

weight   friction

FLOAT THAT BOAT

Boats are remarkable because they can float. But how does floating work? And how can yachts glide on water without an engine? Splish, splash, let's take the plunge and find out!

gravity

what's the BIG idea?

BUOYANCY

When you put an object in water, **gravity** (the force that makes things fall down to Earth) pulls it down, but the water pushes back. This force is called buoyancy. Buoyancy allows an object to float if its weight is equal to or less than the weight of the water it pushes out of the way.

buoyancy

IN FACT...

SUPER SUBMARINES

Submarines can both float on the surface of water and dive toward the seabed. This is because they contain water tanks. When the tanks are full of water, a submarine is heavy and sinks to the seabed. When the tanks are emptied and filled with air, the submarines become lighter than the water around it and rise to the surface.

MAKE A MODEL YACHT

YOU WILL NEED:

- ✔ An adult helper
- ✔ A plastic bottle
- ✔ A piece of polystyrene (as wide as the bottle)
- ✔ A wooden skewer or plastic straw
- ✔ Scissors
- ✔ Paper
- ✔ Packing tape
- ✔ Tape
- ✔ Cardstock
- ✔ Three small coins
- ✔ Adhesive putty

WARNING! SHARP EDGES!

HOW DOES IT WORK?

Your boat is buoyant—it floats! Try blowing on the sail. Just like a real yacht, the mast and sail turn the blowing force into motion through the water. Experiment by changing the angle of the sail, or design a different-shaped sail. Or you could even make a catamaran (boat with two **hulls**).

1 Ask an adult to help you cut out the middle of the plastic bottle. You should add some tape to the cut edge to smooth it off.

2 Make sure the lid is secure. You can add some putty to secure it.

polystyrene

tape

3 Place the polystyrene in the middle of the bottle, and secure it with packing tape.

4 Cut the paper into a triangle, place the skewer or straw in the middle, and tape it to the paper. Fold the triangle over the skewer or straw, and seal it with tape to make the sail.

tape

fold

crease

5 Fold a piece of cardstock in half, and draw this shape (left). Cut out the shape (cutting through both layers of cardstock).

6 Open the card, and tape a coin to each side. Refold the card and tape it together—this will be your keel, which keeps the boat stable. Fold the tabs outward.

tab

taped coin

fold

tab

tape

keel

tape   **tape**

7 Tape the tabs of the keel to the base of the boat. Wrap packing tape around the outside of the bottom of the keel to make it more water resistant.

8 Push the mast and sail into the polystyrene. Get set for a grand launching ceremony! Why not add some cargo to test out its buoyancy?

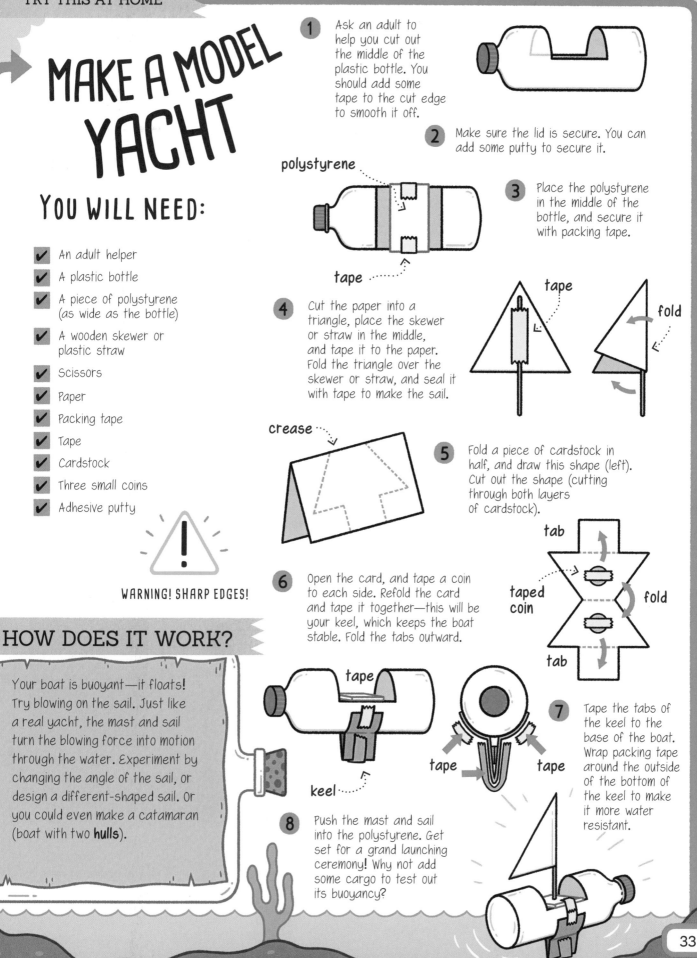

SUPER SPEEDY BOATS

What's that? The wind isn't blowing and your boat is stuck? No problem, techies—let's find a different way to power your boat. In addition to the wind, boats can be powered by oars, or engines that turn propellers.

THE FIRST BOATS

Early boats were powered by wind and sails or by people rowing with oars. As a boat is rowed, the oars push water backward, which in turn thrusts the boat forward. In the first sailboats, the sails blocked the flow of air around them, causing the boats to move at the same speed as the wind pushing them. Sir Isaac Newton's Third Law of Motion explains it all.

oars push water backward

boat moves forward

direction of wind on sail

boat moves forward

what's the BIG idea?

NEWTON'S THIRD LAW OF MOTION

Newton's Third Law of Motion explains that when a force acts in one direction, another force pushes or pulls just as hard in the opposite direction. You can see it everywhere. When you're standing up or sitting down, your body's weight is pressing down on the floor or chair. If the chair or floor didn't push back just as hard, you would fall right through it!

WHO WAS NEWTON?

Sir Isaac Newton (1643–1727) was an English **physicist** who discovered the **Laws of Motion** and made important observations about the force of gravity.

MAKE A JET BOAT

Here's a fun experiment that shows you how jet boats work.

YOU WILL NEED:

- ✔ An adult helper
- ✔ A small (500 ml approx.) plastic bottle with a cap
- ✔ 1 tablespoon of baking soda
- ✔ Vinegar
- ✔ A straw
- ✔ A metal skewer and/or scissors
- ✔ Adhesive putty
- ✔ A small funnel

WARNING! SHARP EDGES!

1. Ask an adult to make a hole in the plastic bottle lid with the skewer and/or scissors.

lid

2. Cut the straw in half. Take one of the halves and push it through the hole in the lid. Seal it with putty.

vinegar

baking soda

3. Place the funnel in the top of the bottle, and carefully pour the vinegar into the bottle until it's about one-quarter full.

4. Stand near a bathtub or a large container filled with water, and pour the baking soda through the funnel into the bottle.

5. Quickly screw the lid onto the bottle, and place the bottle into the water.

6. Stand back and watch!

HOW DOES IT WORK?

The vinegar and baking soda react, producing carbon dioxide gas. Some of the gas goes through the straw and pushes on the water. The water pushes back, and the boat moves forward in the opposite direction of the gas. Yes, it's Newton's Third Law of Motion again!

HOW DOES A MARINE PROPELLER WORK?

Most boats and ships move with **propellers**, which are powered by engines. The propeller creates a rotary (turning) motion that moves the boat forward. Here's how it works.

boat moves forward

1. An engine rotates the propeller shaft
2. Propeller shaft
3. The propeller rotates (turns). Angled blades help to push the water backward.
4. As a result, the boat moves forward. You got it—Newton's Third Law! The force of water pushing backward results in an equal force in the opposite direction.

FEARLESS FLYING

For high-flying techies, the sky's the limit. But how do planes stay up in the sky? What goes up must come down, right? Let's find out.

UP, UP AND AWAY!

Your first challenge is to build a cool paper glider and set it soaring!

YOU WILL NEED:

- ✔ A rectangular piece of heavy paper or cardstock
- ✔ A ruler
- ✔ Tape
- ✔ Scissors
- ✔ A paperclip

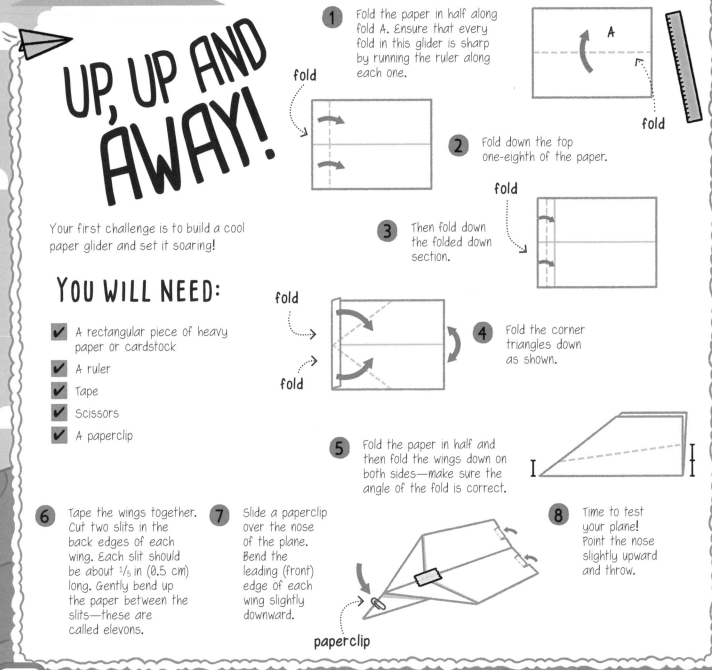

1. Fold the paper in half along fold A. Ensure that every fold in this glider is sharp by running the ruler along each one.

fold

A

fold

2. Fold down the top one-eighth of the paper.

fold

3. Then fold down the folded down section.

fold

fold

4. Fold the corner triangles down as shown.

fold

5. Fold the paper in half and then fold the wings down on both sides—make sure the angle of the fold is correct.

6. Tape the wings together. Cut two slits in the back edges of each wing. Each slit should be about 1/5 in (0.5 cm) long. Gently bend up the paper between the slits—these are called elevons.

7. Slide a paperclip over the nose of the plane. Bend the leading (front) edge of each wing slightly downward.

paperclip

8. Time to test your plane! Point the nose slightly upward and throw.

HOW DOES IT WORK?

The force of your throw pushes the plane forward, and its **streamlined** shape minimizes drag (the force of air pushing against it). The raised elevons help to lift the nose of your plane. Try bending the elevons down and notice how this affects the flight.

elevons

WHAT'S GOING ON?

HOW DO PLANES FLY?

A plane or **glider** can fly because the shape of its wings (known as an **airfoil**) forces air to flow faster over its upper side than its lower side. As a result, the air pressure is lower above the wing and the pressure of the air under the wing creates a force called **lift** that keeps the plane airborne. The propeller, powered by an engine, forces the plane forward.

FORCES THAT AFFECT FLIGHT

4 Lift keeps the plane airborne.

2

3 The engine and propeller power the plane forward.

4

2 Drag acts to slow the plane.

1 Gravity pulls the plane down.

WHO WERE THE WRIGHT BROTHERS?

Orville (1871–1948) and Wilbur (1867–1912) Wright were American inventors. They built and flew the first successful powered aircraft in 1903. They tested every part of their plane and flew it first as a glider and then with an engine and propeller.

JUMPING JET POWER

Propeller planes are fast and furious but military planes and space explorers need to go faster. A LOT FASTER! So how about a blast of jet power? Fasten your safety belts!

VROOOOOOOOOOOMMMMMM!

TRY THIS AT HOME

THREE-SECOND EXPERIMENT

Welcome to the fastest, funniest experiment in the book. All you need is a balloon—and a good pair of lungs!

YOU WILL NEED:

- ✔ A balloon
- ✔ Yourself!

HUFF!

PUFF!

2 Let it go!

1 Blow up the balloon.

WEEEEEEEEEEEEEEEEEEE

HOW DOES IT WORK?

Sir Isaac Newton's very useful Third Law of Motion is hard at work! The air blasting out from the balloon when you let it go creates an opposite force that pushes the balloon forward. A similar motion occurs in planes with jet engines.

balloon forward →

air out ←

HOW DOES A JET ENGINE WORK?

Most modern aircraft are powered by jet engines. These engines burn liquid fuel to produce a powerful forward force called thrust. Let's take a look.

1. Cold air flows into the engine.

4. The hot gas blast turns **turbines**.

5. The blast shoots out of the rear. The engine is pushed forward.

engine moves forward

2. Rotors squeeze air to raise its pressure and temperature.

3. In the combustion chamber, the air is sprayed with fuel and an electric spark makes the mixture explode.

IN FACT...

SPEEDY JETS

The fastest piloted jet ever was the US X-15. It flew at 6.7 times the speed of sound—that's 4,500 miles (7,200 km) per hour and about 5 ½ hours to fly around the earth.

BOOM!

TRY THIS AT HOME

TAKE A SPIN

Let's see what jet power can do when you find it at home.

YOU WILL NEED:

- ✔ A bendy straw
- ✔ A pencil with an eraser on the end
- ✔ A pin
- ✔ A balloon
- ✔ Tape
- ✔ Scissors

1 Bend the straw so that the bendable part is at a right angle to the rest of the straw.

2 Blow up the balloon a few times to make it saggy, and tape it to the end of the straw.

3 Pin the straw to the eraser. In order to balance the balloon's weight, the pin should be closer to the bent end of the straw than to the balloon. Push the pin firmly into the eraser.

4 Blow up the balloon through the straw. Hold the pencil tight and let the air escape from the balloon.

HOW DOES IT WORK?

The balloon should whiz around in a circle. Jet engines are tightly attached to the wings, or the body of the plane, to ensure that their power is directed behind the plane.

MIGHTY MICROBES

Technology isn't always about machines. Biotechnology is a type of technology that uses living things to invent new stuff. Sounds impossible? Not in the world of biotechnology!

what's the BIG idea?

BIOTECHNOLOGY

Biotechnology is not exactly new—we've been breeding animals, growing plants, and baking bread for centuries. In bread making, microbes (tiny living things) called yeast are added to flour dough. The yeast produces carbon dioxide gas as it feeds off the simple sugars in the flour, which makes the bread rise when it's baked.

The ancient Assyrians and Egyptians used yeast to make bread thousands of years ago.

TRY THIS AT HOME

YUMMY YOGURT

Making yogurt is traditional biotechnology that relies on microbes called **bacteria**. Mm-mm-mm—now that sure is tasty technology!

YOU WILL NEED:

- ✔ An adult helper
- ✔ A bowl
- ✔ A clean cloth
- ✔ A wooden spoon
- ✔ A pot
- ✔ A cooking thermometer
- ✔ A measuring cup
- ✔ 17 fl oz (500 ml) milk
- ✔ 4 tablespoons of plain live yogurt
- ✔ A stove or hot plate

WARNING! HOT POT!

1. Pour the milk into the pot. Ask an adult to gently heat it to around 185°F (85°C). Check the temperature with the cooking thermometer.

live yogurt

2. Allow the milk to cool to 113°F (45°C) and stir in the live yogurt.

3. Pour the mixture into the bowl and cover it with the clean cloth. Leave the bowl in a warm place until the yogurt has set. This will take about 5–8 hours.

clean cloth

4. Now you can have a taste! Store your yogurt in the fridge.

YUM!

HOW DOES IT WORK?

Milk contains molecules of protein. Heating the milk unravels the rolled-up protein molecules in the liquid. This means the milk forms lumps as it cools. The live yogurt contains two **species** (types) of bacteria that feed on sugar in the milk, converting it to **lactic acid**. The acid gives yogurt its distinctive, slightly sharp taste—so many people sweeten it with fruit or honey.

a close-up of yogurt bacteria

base pair

what's the BIG idea?

GENES AND GENETIC ENGINEERING

Living things consist of microscopic building blocks called cells, which contain molecules of a **compound** called deoxyribonucleic acid—or DNA for short. DNA contains pairs of smaller molecules called base pairs.

The sequence of base pairs is an instruction code for how the cell should behave. A length of DNA that codes for a particular feature, such as eye color, is called a gene. By altering this code, techies change what it does. This is called genetic engineering. An example of this is changing the DNA in crops to make them resistant to disease caused by insects.

a DNA molecule

PUZZLE ZONE

FIND THE GENE CODE

In this puzzle, two code strips (below) are the DNA of MOM and DAD. If both strips have TAAT, their baby will have blue eyes. If CGGC is in one or both strips, their baby will have brown eyes. What color eyes does their baby have?

MOM = ATCGTAGCATTACGCGGCGCGCATATACGCG
DAD = GCCGCGATTACGGCATATTATAGCGCCGTATA

LET IT GROW!

You might think that farming has nothing to do with techie stuff like gadgets, computers, or robots—but think again! Farming also uses technology, so let's get to grips with growing greens techie style!

WHAT'S THE BIG IDEA?

AGRICULTURAL TECHNOLOGY

Ever since some unknown ancient person planted a seed and munched the first home-grown salad, people have been growing plants for food. Every invention for growing plants and raising animals, including tools, machines, containers and systems for watering, and gathering and storing crops, is technology.

watermelon

corn

wheat

SOME OF THE FIRST CROPS, STILL GROWN TODAY

IN FACT...

THROUGH THE AGES...

1. Crop growing was developed in various parts of the world from about 9500 BCE. Soon after, people raised livestock and built water channels to water plants, in a process known as irrigation.

3. In the 1900s, German scientists discovered how to use nitrogen gas from air, combined with hydrogen gas, to make ammonia-based fertilizers (substances that help to make soil more fertile for growing crops).

2. Until the 1800s, farming depended on muscle power. Afterward, steam- and petrol-powered machines became widespread. Petrol tractors were developed in 1901.

HOW DOES A HYDROPONIC PLANT SYSTEM WORK?

Believe it or not, plants don't need soil! All they need is moisture and **minerals** and for their roots to be supported. Hydroponics is a technology used for growing plants in containers without soil. In this way, plant watering and feeding can be controlled easily and monitored for the best results.

HYDROPONIC SYSTEM

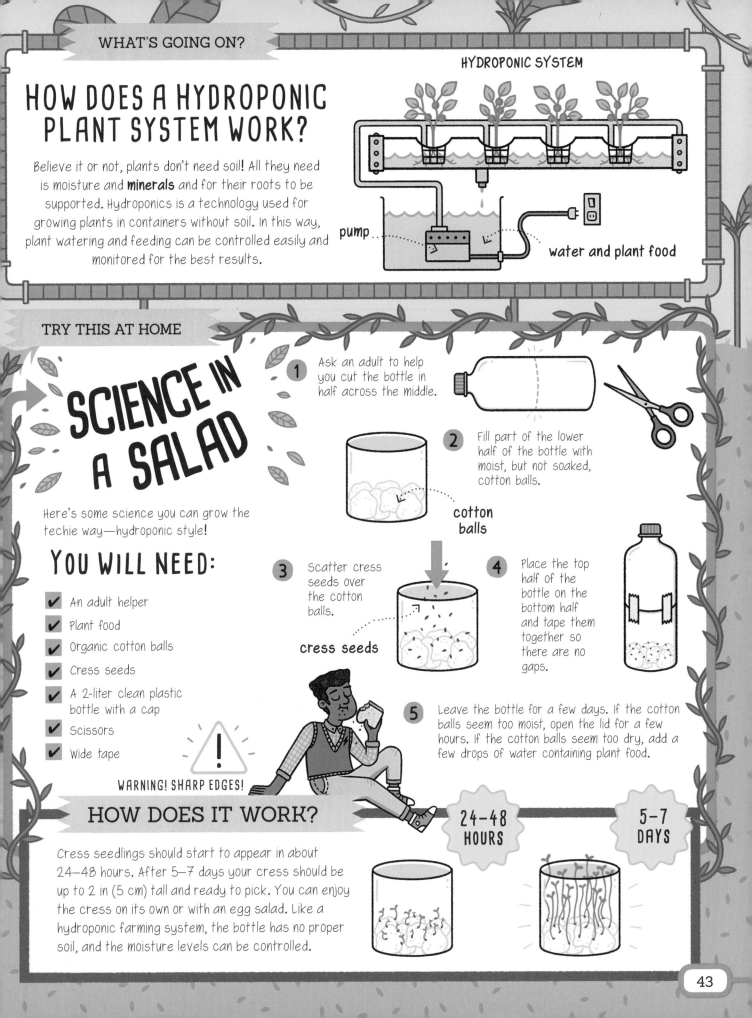

pump

water and plant food

TRY THIS AT HOME

SCIENCE IN A SALAD

Here's some science you can grow the techie way—hydroponic style!

YOU WILL NEED:

- ✔ An adult helper
- ✔ Plant food
- ✔ Organic cotton balls
- ✔ Cress seeds
- ✔ A 2-liter clean plastic bottle with a cap
- ✔ Scissors
- ✔ Wide tape

⚠ **WARNING! SHARP EDGES!**

1 Ask an adult to help you cut the bottle in half across the middle.

2 Fill part of the lower half of the bottle with moist, but not soaked, cotton balls.

cotton balls

3 Scatter cress seeds over the cotton balls.

cress seeds

4 Place the top half of the bottle on the bottom half and tape them together so there are no gaps.

5 Leave the bottle for a few days. If the cotton balls seem too moist, open the lid for a few hours. If the cotton balls seem too dry, add a few drops of water containing plant food.

HOW DOES IT WORK?

Cress seedlings should start to appear in about 24–48 hours. After 5–7 days your cress should be up to 2 in (5 cm) tall and ready to pick. You can enjoy the cress on its own or with an egg salad. Like a hydroponic farming system, the bottle has no proper soil, and the moisture levels can be controlled.

24–48 HOURS

5–7 DAYS

BRILLIANT BIOMEDICINE

Some techie gadgets are more than cool and better than brilliant—they're lifesaving! Medical technology really is a must-have, so let's look at the intersections between medicine and technology!

WHAT'S THE BIG IDEA?

WHAT IS MEDICAL TECHNOLOGY?

Medical technology is about making machines, products, or systems that can keep us healthy by identifying and curing diseases. It also includes medicines and **implants** that do the job of human body parts.

TRY THIS AT HOME

STRAIGHT FROM THE HEART

This simple medical machine will help you listen to your own heart beating. Or you could try it out on a friend.

YOU WILL NEED:

- ✔ Two small funnels, no bigger than 3 in (6 cm) wide
- ✔ Packaging tape
- ✔ Scissors
- ✔ Plastic tubing
- ✔ A balloon

1 Push each end of the tubing over the neck of the funnels (or the funnel necks over the tubing).

funnel

funnel

tubing

tape

2 Secure the connections tightly with wide tape.

3 Blow up the balloon a few times until it's saggy. Cut off the top third of the balloon, pull it fairly taut, and tape it over the opening of one of your funnels.

packaging tape

4 Place the funnel with the balloon over your bare chest, and listen through the other funnel.

BOOM!

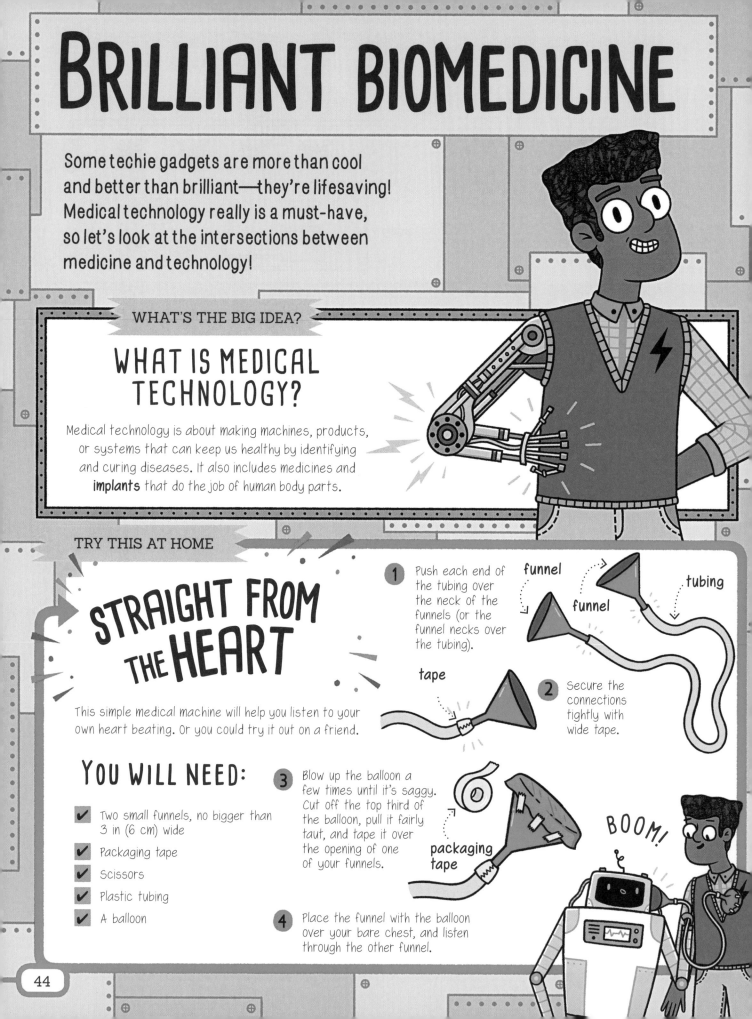

HOW DOES IT WORK?

This is a simple version of a **stethoscope**. You can hear your heart beating (though it can be faint). Like a real stethoscope, a cavity (thin surface with a hollow area behind it) picks up soundwaves, which travel through the tube to your ear. Try timing your heartbeat using a watch with a second hand. Count the beats in 20 seconds. Multiply the number of beats by three to calculate the beats per minute. Run for about a minute and then count your heartbeats again. What's the difference?

HUFF PUFF!

HOW DOES A KIDNEY DIALYSIS MACHINE WORK?

Our kidneys normally filter the waste product **urea** from our blood. If they can't, then a kidney dialysis machine is used to do this vital job instead. Inside the machine, the dialysis fluid absorbs urea from the patient's blood through a thin layer of material called a **membrane**. The fluid also contains **nutrients** that healthy blood needs. If the patient's blood is short of nutrients, they will flow through the membrane and into the patient's blood.

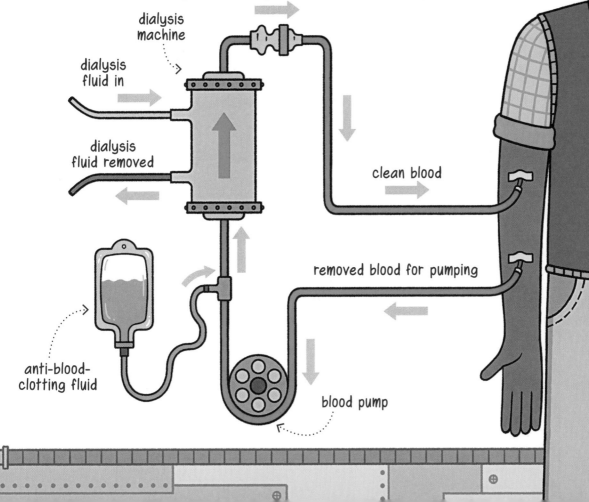

dialysis machine

dialysis fluid in

dialysis fluid removed

clean blood

removed blood for pumping

anti-blood-clotting fluid

blood pump

You've Got the Power

Buzzzz! Where would we be without electricity? Just imagine no heat, no artificial light, and no gadgets to play with. Techies, let's look at how electricity works and how this crucial current reaches us.

what's the BIG idea?

ELECTRICITY

Electricity involves tiny particles that carry electric charge. Particles called **electrons** are found in every atom, and they carry negative electric charge (other particles in atoms, called **protons**, carry positive charge). Electrons can move around, and this movement is an electric **current**. The force to make electrons move can be produced in many ways, often in power stations. Here's how electricity ends up in your gadgets.

1. Electricity is generated in a power station
2. A substation boosts the voltage (the force of the electricity)
3. Pylons carry high voltage electricity
4. A substation reduces the voltage
5. Factories, schools, and hospitals use a lot of electricity
6. Local power line
7. Local substation reduces voltage for homes
8. Electricity is supplied to homes (and your gadgets)

HOW IS ELECTRICITY GENERATED?

In a power station, electric current is produced in a coil as it rotates in a **magnetic field** produced by powerful magnets. The movement energy of the coil is turned into electrical energy. (You'll find more about this on p. 50.)

IN FACT...
BATTERY POWER

Electricity is also produced from batteries. Inside a battery, chemical reactions produce free electrons and a force that pushes the electrons out of one end, the negative electrode. A chemical called an electrolyte allows charges to move inside the battery. When a battery is connected in a circuit (see p. 48), the electrons are forced through the circuit to the positive terminal.

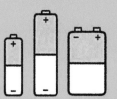

+ positive electrode

- negative (minus) electrode

TRY THIS AT HOME

LEMON BATTERY

Did you know you can create an electric current from a lemon. Yes, really!

YOU WILL NEED:

- ✔ An adult helper
- ✔ A knife
- ✔ Three lemons
- ✔ Three galvanized (zinc-coated) nails
- ✔ Three copper pennies
- ✔ A voltmeter with two leads
- ✔ Two 8 in (20 cm) lengths of plastic-coated copper wire
- ✔ Wire strippers
- ✔ Four alligator clips

1 Roll the lemons on a table so the juices move inside.

slit   slit

2 Ask an adult to strip 1 in (2.5 cm) of plastic coating off both ends of the two wires with wire strippers.

nail   coin

! WARNING! SHARP EDGES!

3 Ask an adult to make two slits in each lemon with a knife, one for a penny and one for a nail.

4 Push one nail and one penny into each lemon.

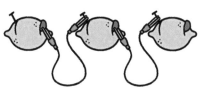

5 Ask an adult to help you connect each of the four ends of copper wire to the alligator clips. Then connect the three lemons to the wires. Each wire should connect to a nail and a penny.

6 Place one lead from your voltmeter onto the remaining penny and one lead onto the remaining nail.

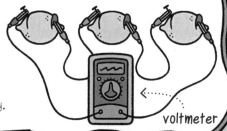

voltmeter

HOW DOES IT WORK?

The lemon juice acts as an electrolyte, and the nails and pennies act as electrodes. When you add the wires, an electric current begins to flow. You can check the voltage of the current on the voltmeter. Why not try it with other fruits and vegetables, such as apples, carrots, or potatoes.

WHO WAS TESLA?

Nikola Tesla (1856–1943) was a physicist and inventor who helped discover and develop the type of electric current that runs into our homes.

A BRIGHT IDEA

HURRAH! So you have electricity in your home! Now let's check out what it can do, by sending it around in a circuit. Yes, techies, we can control the flow of electrical current to power devices. Let's find out how!

TRY THIS AT HOME

BUILD A CIRCUIT

Electricity can flow in a wire if it's got somewhere to go. This is the purpose of an electrical circuit—as you're about to find out.

YOU WILL NEED:

- ✔ An adult helper
- ✔ A small 2 volt flashlight bulb
- ✔ Two AA 1.5 volt batteries
- ✔ Electrical wire (about 12 in/30 cm)
- ✔ Tape
- ✔ Wire strippers

WARNING! BATTERIES MAY GET HOT!

1 Ask an adult to strip ½ in (1 cm) of plastic covering off each end of the wire.

2 Tape one end of the wire to the base (negative end) of a battery.

3 Hold the base of the bulb on the positive end of the battery and touch the other end of the wire to its metal side. The lightbulb should light.

positive end

4 Now tape the positive ends of the two batteries together. Hold the bulb on the negative end of the second battery, and again touch the end of the wire to its metal side.

5 The lightbulb doesn't light! Now for your challenge! Because the bulb lit up at step 3, you know that your equipment is working. How will you change things to make the bulb light?

HOW DOES IT WORK?

The battery, wire, and bulb form a circuit for an electrical circuit to flow through. But the electrons in a circuit will only move from negative areas to positive areas. This means that the electrons are moving from areas where there are lots of them to areas where there aren't. To make the circuit work so the lightbulb lights, you have to connect the negative end of the second battery with the positive end of the first battery.

electrons flow from negative to positive

bulb

plan of a circuit

battery

WHAT'S GOING ON?

HOW DO LIGHTBULBS WORK?

Traditional lightbulbs work like this ...

3) Inert gas in the bulb prevents the filament from burning up.

1) Electric current heats a thin wire called a filament.

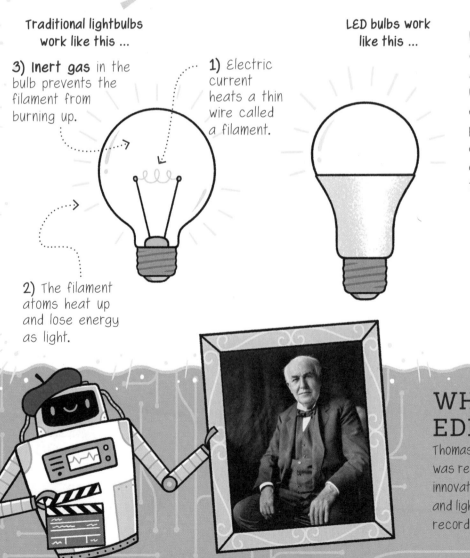

2) The filament atoms heat up and lose energy as light.

LED bulbs work like this ...

LED (light-emitting diode) bulbs work differently from traditional lightbulbs. An LED bulb contains a **semiconductor**—usually made of silicon. It's made up of an electron rich "N" layer and an electron poor "P" layer. An electric current sends electrons into the "P" layer, and the electrons get rid of extra energy in the form of light.

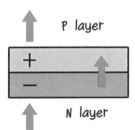

P layer

+

−

N layer

electric current

WHO WAS EDISON?

Thomas Edison (1847–1931) was responsible for over 1,000 innovations including electric bulbs and lighting, movie cameras, and recorded sound.

MAKING MOTORS

OK techies, so the power's up and running and the lights are on. Now let's take a closer look at the connection between electricity and magnetism, and how it's used to build motors. Motors are found in everything from kitchen gadgets and hairdryers to trains.

TRY THIS AT HOME

MAGNETIZE A NAIL

Let's start by observing the amazing connection between electricity and magnetism.

YOU WILL NEED:

- ✔ An adult helper
- ✔ A long nail, made from iron or steel
- ✔ One AA 1.5 volt battery
- ✔ A long piece of plastic-coated copper wire
- ✔ Wire strippers
- ✔ Tape
- ✔ A small paper clip

⚠️

WARNING! BATTERY MAY GET HOT!

1. Ask an adult to strip ¾ in (2 cm) of plastic coating from each end of the wire with wire strippers.

2. Wrap the wire tightly around the nail at least 30 times, leaving about 12 in (30 cm) of wire on either side. Tape the wire to the nail if necessary to keep the coil in place.

tape

3. Position one end of the wire against one end of the battery and the other wire end to the other end of the battery and tape in place.

4. Now put the point of the nail next to the paper clip, and watch what happens!

HOW DOES IT WORK?

An **electromagnetic force** is electric and magnetic. When the current flows in a wire it produces a magnetic field. This means the nail becomes magnetic and can pick up certain metal objects. Does the number of times the wire is wrapped around the nail make a difference to the magnetism?

Electromagnets can be switched on and off and are the basic idea behind an electric motor.
Let's explore.

WHO WAS ØRSTED?

Danish scientist Hans Christian Ørsted (1777–1851) discovered the link between electricity and magnetism. When he ran an electric current close to a **magnetic compass** and the compass needle moved, he realized the current was producing magnetism.

WHAT'S GOING ON?

HOW DOES AN ELECTRIC MOTOR WORK?

Electric motors use electrical power to make things move. They rely on electricity and magnets. Every magnet has a north and a south pole. Magnetic force flows from the north pole to the south pole. That's why north and south poles attract, but two like poles repel.

MAGNETS

N = North   S = South

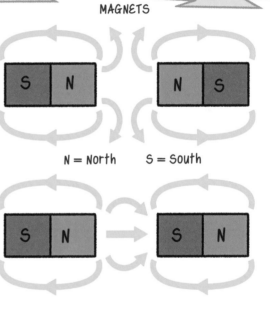

1) An electric motor has a wire loop.

wire loop

commutator

2) An electric current runs through the loop and creates a magnetic field around it. A device called a commutator keeps switching the direction of the current, which constantly reverses the loop's magnetic field.

3) The loop has magnets on either side, and their magnetic fields push and pull the loop, making it spin.

LET'S GET DIGITAL

The latest, up-to-the minute electronic gadgets that carry information, such as phones and tablets, depend on digital technology. Traditionally, gadgets sent communication signals with analogue technology. So what's the difference?

TICK, TICK

analogue clock shows time by the position of continuously moving hands

what's the BIG idea?

ANALOGUE
In analogue electronic technology, information is stored as a physical pattern and released as a continuous signal. In an analogue watch, this means the continuous turning of hands usually powered by a battery. In analogue radio, rising and falling sound waves are replicated by continuous rising and falling radio waves (see p. 56) sent through the air.

digital clock shows time as a number that changes at regular intervals

DIGITAL
Digital signals send information as a series of pulses (think of musical notes) that are either "on" or "off." The order of the pulses is a code. Digital machines turn the code into information we can understand. Digital signals are faster than analogue signals and can have fewer errors. Digital gadgets tend to show number displays for readings, such as on a digital watch.

(see p. 56)

PUZZLE ZONE

CAN YOU CRACK THE DIGITAL CODE?

You're a top techie agent. You have received a vital digital code message. But what does it mean? It could be:
S shape = DANGER
V shape = ALL CLEAR
C shape = START NEXT MISSION
Square = RETURN TO BASE

The code is 0000001110010100111000000. The 1s are pulses and the 0s are not.

YOU WILL NEED:

✔ Graph paper
✔ A ruler
✔ A pencil

1 Draw a box that is five squares by five.

2 Each number in the code is a square. Start in the top left square of the box. A 0 = a blank square and a 1 = a square you must fill in. What do you get?

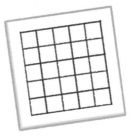

HOW DOES IT WORK?

The code is a type of digital code called binary code—the 1 is an "on" signal and the 0 is an "off" signal. Most computers use binary code to process information. But what does your binary code message mean? Check the back of the book to find out.

> 0000001110010
> 100111000000

WHAT'S GOING ON?

HOW DOES OPTICAL FIBER WORK?

When you call a friend on a landline you're probably signaling to him/her using bursts of light! That's because optical fiber phone lines transmit messages as pulses of light fired from lasers (beams of light). The information that optical fiber cables transmit tends to be digital, such as fast speed internet connections.

1) Optical fiber phone lines are made of very thin strands of pure glass.

2) A pulse of light reflects inside a strand. The light is reflected back from the surface of the glass and cannot escape.

IN FACT...

OPTICAL FIBER

- One optical fiber is ten times thinner than a human hair.
- An optical fiber could carry a signal around Earth in less than one second.

WHO WAS KAPANY?

Indian-born American physicist Narinder Singh Kapany (b. 1926) was one of the first to transmit a good picture through a large bundle of optical fibers in the 1950s.

CLEVER COMPUTERS

Techies and computers are a perfect match! We can't get enough of them—so get set for a techie treat. We're about to discover the wonders of computers!

microprocessor

WHAT'S THE BIG IDEA?

HOW DO COMPUTERS WORK?

A computer is a machine that takes the information you put into it, stores it, organizes it (processes it), and allows you to alter it and then access it. Putting information into a computer is called input, storing it is called memory, altering information is called processing, and accessing it is called output.

The instructions are called software and the physical pieces that do the work are called hardware.

Input hardware includes a keyboard and a mouse. Output hardware includes a monitor and often a printer.

monitor

camera

keyboard

mouse

printer

WHAT'S GOING ON?

HOW DOES A MOUSE WORK?

A computer mouse contains sensors (like we have eyes or ears) that detect the movement of your hand and then sends signals to the computer to move a pointer on the screen. In the past, mice had wires connected to the computers. Now mice tend to be wireless, and signals are sent via radio or infrared waves (see p. 56).

wireless mouse

wired mouse

EARLY COMPUTERS

- The first electronic computer was called ENIAC (right). It weighed 27 tons—more than 10 cars—and took up a whole room. In 2015, scientists built a computer that could balance on the edge of a nickel!

- The first computer mouse was wooden. Now there are computer mice in every material you can imagine. And some computers can be controlled by hand gestures.

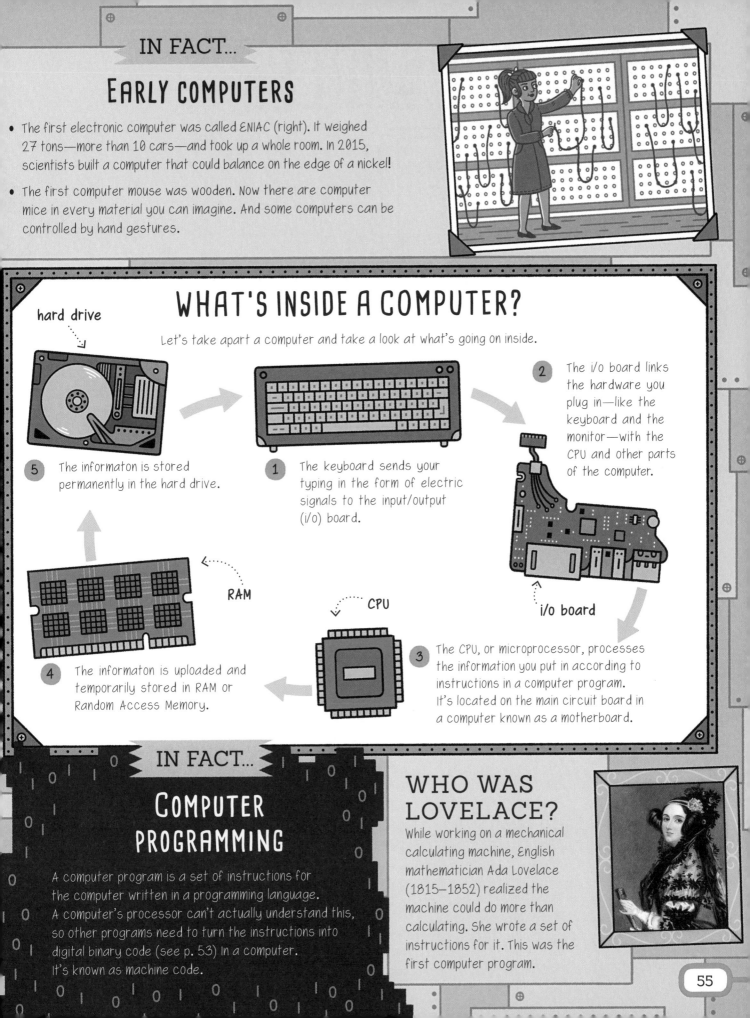

WHAT'S INSIDE A COMPUTER?

Let's take apart a computer and take a look at what's going on inside.

hard drive

5 The informaton is stored permanently in the hard drive.

1 The keyboard sends your typing in the form of electric signals to the input/output (i/o) board.

2 The i/o board links the hardware you plug in—like the keyboard and the monitor—with the CPU and other parts of the computer.

i/o board

RAM

CPU

4 The informaton is uploaded and temporarily stored in RAM or Random Access Memory.

3 The CPU, or microprocessor, processes the information you put in according to instructions in a computer program. It's located on the main circuit board in a computer known as a motherboard.

COMPUTER PROGRAMMING

A computer program is a set of instructions for the computer written in a programming language. A computer's processor can't actually understand this, so other programs need to turn the instructions into digital binary code (see p. 53) In a computer. It's known as machine code.

WHO WAS LOVELACE?

While working on a mechanical calculating machine, English mathematician Ada Lovelace (1815–1852) realized the machine could do more than calculating. She wrote a set of instructions for it. This was the first computer program.

LOOK, NO WIRES!

Modern devices can send messages through empty space without wires. How do they do this? They use waves instead. Let's investigate!

what's the BIG idea?

ELECTROMAGNETIC WAVE

electric force

magnetic force

WAVES OF ENERGY

Charged particles release energy as electricity and magnetism in electromagnetic waves, also known as **radiation.** Light is an electromagnetic wave, and there are other types of electromagnetic waves that you can't see.

WHAT'S GOING ON?

ELECTROMAGNETIC SPECTRUM

The different types of electromagnetic waves have differing wavelengths and frequencies. Wavelength is the distance from the peak of one wave to the peak of the next one. Frequency is the measure of how often a wave repeats. All of these waves make up the electromagnetic spectrum. Phones, televisions, and radios use signals made up of electromagnetic waves. So do **X-ray** machines and microwave ovens.

RADIO WAVES	MICROWAVES	INFRARED	VISIBLE LIGHT	ULTRAVIOLET	X-RAYS	GAMMA RAYS
Transmit TV and radio signals	Used in cell phone calls, ready meals, weather forecasting	Zaps through TV remotes, security alarms, toasters	Light waves enable you to see things	Fluorescent lightbulbs, detecting forged bank notes	Used in X-ray photographs	Used to kill bacteria and cancer cells

← LOW-ENERGY WAVELENGTH   HIGH-ENERGY WAVELENGTH →

IN FACT...

RADIO AND TV

How are radio and TV programs transmitted by electromagnetic waves? Sounds and pictures are turned into electrical signals that a radio transmitter then sends out as radio waves. The waves are picked up by radio receivers, which turn radio waves into electrical currents. These are then turned back into the original sounds or pictures. Wireless devices like routers, printers, and laptops use radio waves to transmit data messages.

radio waves are transmitted and received

BE AN ELECTROMAGNETIC WAVE DETECTIVE

Your challenge is to identify devices that use different electromagnetic waves.

YOU WILL NEED:

☑ A big sheet of paper
☑ Colored pencils or pens

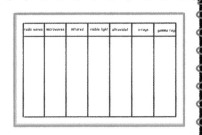

1 Divide the paper into seven columns. Write the name of the seven different types of electromagnetic waves at the top of each column.

radio waves	microwaves	infrared	visible light	ultraviolet	x-rays	gamma rays

2 Study the electromagnetic spectrum chart on p.56. In each column on your chart, draw in examples of how each type of wave is used. For instance, under Infrared, draw a TV remote.

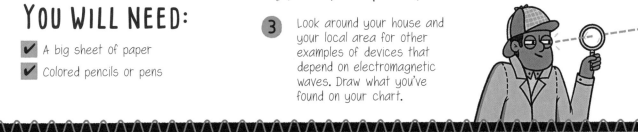

3 Look around your house and your local area for other examples of devices that depend on electromagnetic waves. Draw what you've found on your chart.

IN FACT...

WIRELESS WONDERS

Satnav (or **satellite** navigation) systems use radio waves to help you find your location. A radio receiver in your car's satnav system picks up signals from three or four satellites orbiting Earth. The signals from the satellites give details of their positions and the time. The receiver in your car then compares the signals to figure out where you are.

Not all wireless technology depends on radio waves. TV remote controls, for instance, shine infrared light at a detector to operate something. Infrared light consists of electromagnetic waves we can't see but we can sometimes feel as heat. Any warm object gives off infrared waves—even you!

WHO WAS HERTZ?

Heinrich Rudolf Hertz (1857–1894) was a German physicist who proved the existence of the electromagnetic spectrum.

THE INCREDIBLE INTERNET

The Internet has everything that anyone can imagine—every type of information, fun, shopping, news, movies, and TV. But how does this worldwide wonder work?

HOW DOES THE INTERNET WORK?

The Internet is a worldwide network linking electronic devices, such as computers and smartphones. Every device has an address called an IP (Internet Protocol) address. It allows one device to communicate with another over the Internet according to set rules.

1) A computer sends a message asking for a web page. The message is called a packet.

2) The packet is processed by routers and servers (large computers that sort out requests and deliveries of data) and guided across the world by fiber optic cables or satellites.

Every message on the Internet carries the sender's IP address, the IP address it is sent to, and instructions for assembling the packets. So, even if a device is shared by people with different names and e-mail addresses, the information can get to the right place.

3) An Internet server computer receives the message.

4) A web page is broken down into many packets and sent back in the same way.

5) A computer assembles packets and shows a web page on your screen.

58

PLAY THE INTERNET GAME

① All three players sit around a table with pens and paper.

② Player A goes out of the room.

Here's how to bring the Internet into your own home WITHOUT even switching on a computer!

YOU WILL NEED:

- ✔ Three friends (including you)
- ✔ Pieces of paper
- ✔ Pens

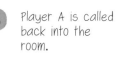

③ Player B thinks of an animal. He or she whispers the name of the animal to Player C.

④ Player C draws a picture of the animal, then rips the drawing into four equal pieces.

⑤ Player A is called back into the room.

⑥ Player B hands the pieces to Player A.

⑦ Player A puts the pieces together and tries to guess the animal. Did he or she get it right?

⑧ Repeat the game several times so that each player tries a different role.

HOW DOES IT WORK?

This game is fun, but it also tells us a bit about how the Internet works.

Player B is like an Internet user. The request for a picture of an animal is like a request for a web page.

Player C is like an Internet server that receives the request and breaks down the web page into packets.

Player A is like Player B's computer. It puts the packets together to form a web page.

THE FANTASTIC PHONE

Many people would be lost without their cell phones, but it takes a true techie to figure out how they work!

→ what's the **BIG** idea?

HOW DO CELL PHONES WORK?

A cell phone is both a radio transmitter and a receiver. Due to its small **antenna** and battery, a cell phone can't send a signal very far—but a wireless connection between individual phones, known as a phone network, solves that problem.

2) A **microchip** (tiny electrical circuit) turns your voice into a binary code.

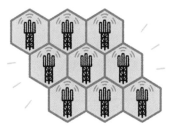

3) A radio transmitter in your phone sends out the code as a radio wave. The radio wave reaches the nearest phone tower.

1) A microphone converts sound waves from your voice into electric signals.

HELLO!

The area of land covered by a cell phone network is often divided into hexagonal-shaped cells. This is so it can cover a maximum area without overlaps. Each cell has a phone tower and a base station. Antennae on the tower pick up radio signals from your phone, and the base station routes them to the base station nearest to the person you are calling.

4) The phone tower passes the signals on to a base station.

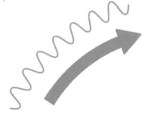

HELLO!

5) The base station forwards the message. It's picked up by the radio receiver in the phone of the person you are calling.

RADIO WAVE BLOCKER

Have you noticed that you sometimes lose reception on your phone or car radio when you go into a tunnel? That's because the radio waves have been blocked and can't get through to your receiver. In this activity you can use a radio-controlled car and remote to test out which materials block radio waves.

YOU WILL NEED:

- ✔ A radio-controlled toy car and remote
- ✔ A pen
- ✔ Paper
- ✔ Aluminum foil
- ✔ Fabric
- ✔ A plastic bag

1 Draw a chart with three columns. Write "Material" at the top of the first column, "Does the car move?" at the top of the second, and "What happened?" at the top of the third.

Material	Does the car move?	What happened?
Aluminum foil		
Paper		
Fabric		
Plastic bag		

2 In the "Material" column write "Aluminum foil," "Paper," "Fabric," and "Plastic bag."

3 Try covering the remote control in the aluminum foil. Make sure you wrap it around several times so the remote is completely covered.

foil

4 Try working the remote to move the car. Does it still work? Write your result in the chart.

5 Now repeat step 3 with each of the other materials one at a time and write your results in the chart. What did you find?

HOW DOES IT WORK?

Did you manage to make the car move when the remote was covered in aluminum foil or any of the other materials? The remote works as a transmitter of radio waves, which the car receives as an instruction to move. If something blocks the transmitter on the remote, then the signal won't get through. You probably found that the lighter materials did not block the radio waves but the aluminum foil did. This is because aluminum, like other metals, blocks and reflects radio waves.

SUPER SMART MACHINES

Machines work hard, but they don't have brains. Techies have been developing machines with what's known as artificial intelligience. Let's explore what's special about these clever machines.

what's the BIG idea?

ARTIFICIAL INTELLIGENCE

Artificial intelligence (AI) is an area of computer technology that aims to build machines that can think and solve problems in a similar way to animals, including humans. These thinking machines will need skills, such as **reasoning**, planning, and learning. Let's look at some of the ways that artificial intelligence has been developed in cars, chatbots, and games.

DRIVERLESS CARS

These cars don't need humans to control them. They have electronic sensors that help detect obstacles in their path. They use satellite navigation to find their way.

CHATBOTS

Chatbots are computer programs that can have simple conversations with humans. They learn how humans talk and what words are commonly used. They are often found in customer service—they help explain things on a website or they give instructions on how to use something technical.

COMPUTER CHAMPIONS

Computers have been programmed to play board games, such as chess and AlphaGo, without human help. They have won against human players several times. But computers cannot be traditionally programmed to play the game of Go. It took until 2016 for an AI program to beat Go Top Don (grandmaster) Lee Sedol.

TREASURE HUNT ALGORITHM

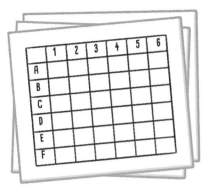

1 You and your friend should both draw three plans as shown, each on a separate sheet of paper.

When you use an Internet search engine, you use instructions called algorithms to find data that you are looking for without any human help. Here's a game that helps you plan your own treasure-hunting search algorithm.

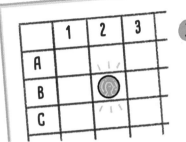

2 Ask your friend to take one plan into another room with the coins, and place one coin on any square he/she likes until all the coins have been used up.

YOU WILL NEED:

- ✔ A friend
- ✔ Six coins
- ✔ Two pencils
- ✔ Two rulers
- ✔ Six sheets of paper

3 Using one of your plans, try to guess where your friend placed his/her coins. If A1 is your first guess write "1" in that square. If your guess is correct, draw a circle in the same box. If it's wrong, write an X. Keep guessing until you find all the coins.

4 Repeat the game (using different plans) but this time, after your guess, your friend must tell you the location of another square WITHOUT coins. Mark that square with an X on your plan.

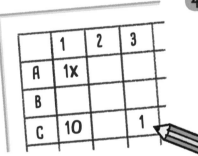

HOW DOES IT WORK?

Steps 3, 4, and 5 represent different search algorithms for finding coins. In step 3, you chose random squares. Unless you're very lucky, it will be slower than step 4, which uses an algorithm that reviews two sets of data—positive and negative. Step 5 should be quickest because it uses an algorithm in which you review all the data at once, and it gives you a clue where to look.

5 Repeat the game a third time. This time your friend starts by telling you the rows where coins are placed in numerical order. So, if the coins are hidden in A4, B3, C5, D1, E2, F6 your friend will say: D, E, B, A, C, F. Where two letters have the same number, they can be given in any order.

RESTLESS ROBOTS

Robots are incredible machines that can be programmed to perform useful work for us. Some have even saved lives by helping surgeons perform medical operations.

HOW DO ROBOT ARMS WORK?

Most robots have moving parts, and many are designed to work in factories, **welding**, painting, packaging, or assembling products. They are controlled by computers and powered by motors and can move continuously—only stopping when they need servicing.

Most robots have a jointed arm that can move in three ways: yawing (moving side to side), rolling (rotating), and pitching (moving up and down). They have sensors that make sure the arms move just the right amount.

2) roll (rotation)

view from side

3) pitch (up and down)

view from side

1) yawing (side to side)

view from above

HELPFUL ROBOTS

Robots also do dangerous jobs that humans can't do—like cleaning up dangerous waste, disposing of unexploded bombs, rescuing people from rubble after an earthquake, or working in extreme environments, such as in space or deep underwater.

bomb disposal robot

robot arm used in space

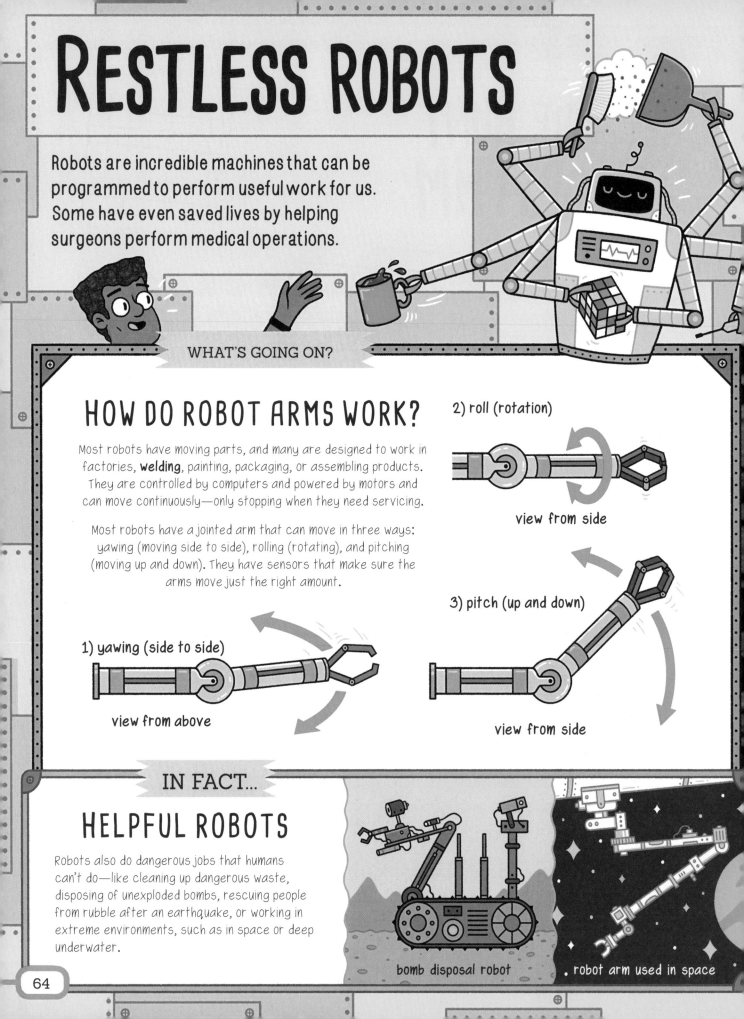

MAKE A ROBOT ARM

So could you build a robot arm? Go on—it's easier than it looks.

YOU WILL NEED:

- ✔ An adult helper
- ✔ Medium-weight cardboard
- ✔ Skewer or scissors (for making holes)
- ✔ A ruler
- ✔ 7 paper fasteners
- ✔ A pencil
- ✔ Glue or tape

1 Cut the cardboard into seven ³/₄ x 6 in (2 x 15 cm) sticks. Cut one stick in half.

1 1 2 2 3 3

hole

2 Make holes in the sticks as shown. Each hole must be big enough for a paper fastener to pass through and be able to rotate.

3 Assemble the robot arm using the sticks marked 1, 2, 3 connected with paper fasteners as shown. Once a paper fastener is pushed through two sticks, push the arms down on the other side so that the sticks can't come apart.

1 2 3
1 2 3

4 Finally, glue or tape the two half sticks to the ends of sticks 3 as shown.

TOP

¹/₂ sticks

HOW DOES IT WORK?

Your robot arm has limited movement but it should be able to pick up small objects. A digital robot arm would be connected to a computer with a program telling it what to do.

PUZZLE ZONE
ROBOT RIVALRY

Out of the following activities, which ones do you think a robot would do better than a human? Which activities do you think will always be done better by humans?

1) Running a race
2) Cooking
3) Solving a Rubik's cube puzzle
4) Picking apples
5) Writing poetry
6) Swimming underwater
7) Copying human handwriting
8) Performing magic tricks
9) Assembling DIY furniture
10) Telling jokes

ANSWERS ARE AT THE BACK OF THE BOOK

MEET MY ROBOT!

While many robot jobs are mechanical, robot programming is extending into the realms of the senses (hearing and speech) and reasoning. With further research, robots will have touching capabilities, too!

→ ## what's the BIG idea?

ROBOT TRAINING

Although most robots are programmable machines that work in industry, some, especially those built to interact with people, are designed to look like us. We wonder how many human things they'll eventually be able to do. Our first job has been to train them; now robots have the capability of programming and training each other.

PUZZLE ZONE

ROBOT TRAINING CHALLENGE

Can you train your robot to pick up your cell phone and bring it to your chair? The room is divided into squares, each with a grid reference.

Key

🤖	robot
🪑	chair
📱	phone
*	to
P/G	pick or give

	1	2	3	4	5
A					📱
B					
C					
D					
E	🤖	🪑			

Here's the algorithm (instruction) that tells the robot what to do:

> 🤖 * C1 * C5 * A5 P/G 📱 * A4 * E4 * E2 P/G 📱

Notice how * appears whenever the robot changes direction. The robot can't move diagonally. Can you rewrite the algorithm with fewer changes of direction?

66

ANSWERS ARE AT THE BACK OF THE BOOK

BUILD A ROBOT HAND

Before you can train your robot for tricky tasks, you need to design a more advanced hand.

YOU WILL NEED:

- ✔ Cardboard
- ✔ Five straws
- ✔ A pencil
- ✔ Scissors
- ✔ String
- ✔ Tape
- ✔ A ruler with metric and imperial measurements

1 Trace your hand (with your fingers separated a little) and wrist on the cardboard. Then using a ruler, make the outlines of your fingers thicker and straighter.

2 Cut out the hand and arm.

3 Cut four straws into three 1-cm pieces and one 4-cm piece (for the fingers). Then cut one straw into two 1-cm pieces and one 3-cm piece (for the thumb).

4 Draw three horizontal lines at intervals on the fingers and two on the thumb. Make folds at the lines.

5 Tape the straw pieces to the hand at intervals as shown.

tape

6 Cut the string into five pieces. The pieces should be longer than the length of the hand and wrist.

7 Thread the string pieces through the straws. Tape the string ends securely to the top of the fingers.

8 Now hold all the strings together at the bottom of the hand, and try pulling on the strings. Look what happens!

HOW DOES IT WORK?

Robot hands are often designed to work like human hands. In a human hand, flexible tissue called tendons pull on your finger bones. The straws and strings work like bones and tendons.

tendon (white)

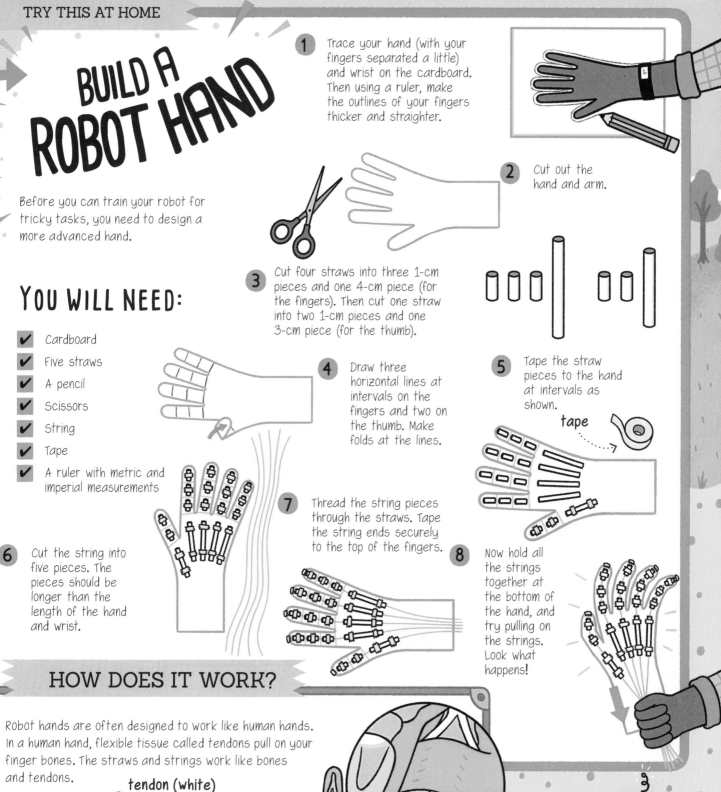

OUT OF THIS WORLD

Beyond our planet, there are new worlds to discover. They may hold the key to new scientific discoveries that will help humans continue to flourish. So let's investigate space exploration technology.

what's the BIG idea?

SPACE EXPLORATION

Space exploration involves some incredibly advanced technology, including radio-controlled **space probes** that fly past planets taking photographs and temperatures, space stations that orbit the earth, and roving robots that explore the moon and Mars. Rockets take all these machines to their destinations.

Space rovers are robots that explore other planets in conditions that humans are not able to survive in. For instance, Mars Rovers are robots that collect rocks and take pictures to establish whether Mars may have once been home to living things, or if it could be again.

The International Space Station (ISS) is a satellite that orbits 240 miles (390 km) above Earth at a speed of 5 miles (7.66 km) per second. Here, astronaut scientists carry out research into how living things can stay alive and healthy in space.

Rockets are propelled into space by the hot gas blasted out as a result of burning fuel. Yes, it's Newton's Third Law of Motion again! We will need rockets that can carry bigger loads if we want to travel farther into space because we'll require more supplies.

MAKE AN AIR-PRESSURE ROCKET

Want to make a rocket without an enormous explosion? You're in luck. We can force gas out of a rocket without burning fuel. We do need two of the same ingredients, though: gas and pressure, the pushing force that expels the gas. Our gas will be air, and we will use a bottle to create the pressure.

YOU WILL NEED:

✔ An adult helper
✔ A straw (cut off any bendy parts)
✔ Two pieces of paper
✔ Tape
✔ A large plastic bottle with a cap
✔ Glue or modeling clay
✔ A metal skewer
✔ Scissors

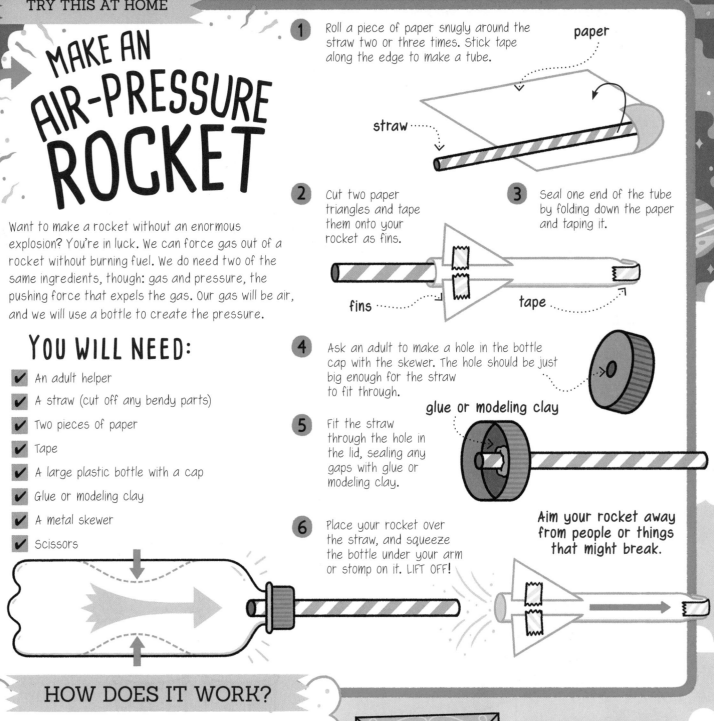

1. Roll a piece of paper snugly around the straw two or three times. Stick tape along the edge to make a tube.

paper

straw

2. Cut two paper triangles and tape them onto your rocket as fins.

fins

3. Seal one end of the tube by folding down the paper and taping it.

tape

4. Ask an adult to make a hole in the bottle cap with the skewer. The hole should be just big enough for the straw to fit through.

glue or modeling clay

5. Fit the straw through the hole in the lid, sealing any gaps with glue or modeling clay.

6. Place your rocket over the straw, and squeeze the bottle under your arm or stomp on it. LIFT OFF!

Aim your rocket away from people or things that might break.

HOW DOES IT WORK?

The air from the bottle is pushed into the paper rocket, but the rocket doesn't have space for all of it. Air is forced backward out of the rocket, creating the opposite, forward-pushing force known as thrust.

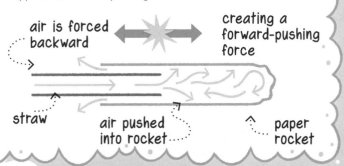

air is forced backward

creating a forward-pushing force

straw

air pushed into rocket

paper rocket

WHO WAS GODDARD?

Robert H. Goddard (1882–1945) was an American inventor who launched the first liquid-fueled rocket in 1926 and came up with the idea of rocket jet propulsion.

SUPER SPACE SUITS

Astronauts have to face the challenges of living in space, where there's no oxygen to breathe, no water, and home is a distant blue planet. Their clothes are their portable living environment.

→ what's the BIG idea?

HOW DOES A SPACE SUIT WORK?

A space suit has many devices to help astronauts survive in space. It supplies oxygen so they can breathe and takes away carbon dioxide that they breathe out. It has many layers to protect them from flying debris (space rocks or garbage left over from other spacecraft), to maintain air pressure inside (as there's no air in space), to withstand extreme heat and cold, and to protect them from the sun's harmful rays and winds.

Helmet has a sun visor and a camera

Astronaut communicates using a radio microphone and headphones

Oxygen is supplied to helmet

Hard protective outer layer

Backpack has oxygen and power batteries

Undersuit has water-filled pipes to cool the suit

Controls for oxygen, cooling system, and radio

IN FACT...

SPACE TOILETS

How do astronauts go to the bathroom in space? They sit on toilets that work a bit like vacuum cleaners—they suck all the waste away!

WHAT'S GOING ON?

WEIGHTLESSNESS

When you've seen pictures of astronauts, have you noticed that they bounce around "weightless" in their spacecraft? That's because they are in free-fall. Gravity is making them fall to Earth but because the spacecraft is falling too, it looks like the astronauts are floating. At the same time, the spacecraft is orbiting Earth at high speed, which prevents it from falling down to Earth.

IN FACT...

MASS OR WEIGHT?

Weight and mass are not exactly the same thing. Strictly speaking, weight is the force of gravity on something, and it varies at different locations. Mass, however, is the amount of **matter** in something and it always stays the same.

mass   weight

TRY THIS AT HOME

SPACE WEIGHT CHALLENGE

Did you know that you would weigh less on the moon? That's because the force of gravity on the moon is less than that on Earth. Let's pretend you're a space explorer who needs to figure out the weight of various things on the moon.

YOU WILL NEED:

✔ Household objects
✔ Paper
✔ A pencil
✔ A weighing scale

1 Collect some household objects—a soccer ball, book, pencil, cell phone.

2 Draw three columns on a sheet of paper. At the top of each column write "Object," "Weight on Earth," and "Weight on Moon."

3 Write the names of the objects you've found under the "Objects" column.

4 Weigh each of the objects on the scale and write their weights in "Weight on Earth" column.

5 Now figure out what each object would weigh on the moon. The force of gravity on the moon is 1/6 of that on Earth, so you'd need to divide your weight on Earth by six.

6 Now write these weights in the "Weight on Moon" column.

IN FACT...

SPACE WORKOUT

Astronauts need to keep fit in order to cope with the physical changes they encounter in space. As there is little gravity in space, their bones and muscles become weaker because they do not have to push back against the force of gravity. On the International Space Station, they regularly exercise so they can keep their bones strong. They run on a special treadmill with a harness so they don't float around, and they use a machine for pushing against weights.

71

PROJECT SPACE STATION

Could we survive in space for longer than a few weeks? Astronauts on the International Space Station (ISS) are using technology to help us explore this question.

what's the BIG idea?

INTERNATIONAL SPACE STATION

On the ISS, astronauts from across the globe examine how living things can survive in space. The ISS is also a testing ground for other spacecraft and systems.

Because there is no natural supply of water on board, water has to be recycled. Every month, an unmanned spacecraft takes supplies, including food, to the ISS.

1) Solar panels—convert sunlight into electricity
2) Radiators—help keep the station at a regular temperature
3) Destiny—US experiment laboratory
4) Harmony—a center for electrical power and electronic data
5) Russian experimental laboratory
6) Columbus—European experiment laboratory
7) Truss—links the different ISS parts together
8) Russian docking point (where spacecraft land)
9) Quest Airlock—main entry and exit point for spacewalks
10) Kibo—Japanese experiment laboratory
11) Zarya—first module to be launched, now used for fuel storage

TRY THIS AT HOME

DESIGN YOUR OWN SPACE STATION

Now's your chance to plan and build your own space station.

1 Take another look at the picture of the ISS and its various parts. Think about which components you'd like in your space station, too. Would you have the same ones?

2 Draw your space station plan on paper and color it in.

3 Now why not build it out of cardboard? What would you call it?

YOU WILL NEED:

- ✔ Paper
- ✔ Colored pencils
- ✔ Tape
- ✔ Scissors
- ✔ Cardboard
- ✔ Optional: aluminum foil, corks, paint

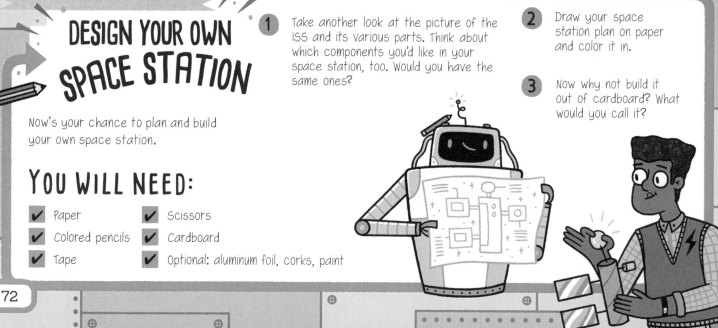

SPACEWALKING

When an astronaut steps outside of a space vehicle it's known as spacewalking. Astronauts on the ISS take spacewalks to carry out experiments, mend parts, and test equipment. They wear space suits and use safety ropes to stay close to the spacecraft. They also wear backpacks with jet thrusters to help them move should they become untethered and need to get back to the station.

WHAT'S GOING ON?

HOW DOES AN AIRLOCK DOOR WORK?

An airlock stops the air from escaping the space station every time an astronaut opens the door. To use it...

1. An astronaut puts on his or her space suit. This contains the air he/she needs to breathe and feel comfortable.

2. The astronaut opens the inner airlock door, goes into the airlock chamber, and then closes the inner airlock door. The inner airlock has the air gradually pumped out of it.

3. The astronaut opens the outer airlock door and has his/her spacewalk. When the astronaut returns, he/she does the whole thing in reverse!

PUZZLE ZONE

AIRLOCK QUIZ

Why aren't astronauts worried about locking themselves out of the airlock door?

a) The key is always strapped to their space suit.

b) There is no key, because there is no lock.

c) The door is voice-activated.

ANSWERS ARE AT THE BACK OF THE BOOK

MAKE A NEW PLANET

Space stations are great for short stays, but what if you want to stay longer in space? What conditions will you need to survive? Let's imagine life on a different planet!

WHAT IS TERRAFORMING?

There are probably billions of planets in our galaxy—but so far we don't know of any apart from Earth that are suitable for life. A planet would need an atmosphere similar to Earth's air so we can breathe. It would also need to be the right temperature. Terraforming is the idea that we can change planets like Venus or Mars to make them more like Earth, so people can live there. The question is, will we be able to build settlements on neighboring planets one day?

TRY THIS AT HOME

PRESSURE PROBLEMS

If the pressure of the gases in a planet's atmosphere is different from the earth's air, it could damage our lungs. This experiment shows you how.

YOU WILL NEED:

- ✔ Small, non-sticky marshmallows
- ✔ A clear, empty wine bottle
- ✔ A vacuum pump for sucking air out of wine bottles

1 Roll the marshmallows into small balls. (If they are sticky, roll them in cornstarch first.)

2 Push the marshmallows into the bottle.

3 Attach the pump, and start pumping out the air. When the marshmallows stop expanding, let the air in.

HOW DOES IT WORK?

As you remove air, the marshmallows expand. They contain air bubbles that seem to grow as the pressure of the surrounding air decreases. If the **atmospheric pressure** of a planet is too low, our lungs can expand in this way without a pressurized suit to keep our bodies in conditions similar to Earth's.

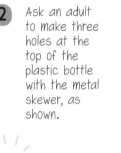

TRY THIS AT HOME

GROWING PLANTS IN SPACE

To live on another planet, we'll need plants to provide food and oxygen. How can we grow plants without a constant supply of nutrients, water, and sunlight? We can create artificial light and recycle nutrients and water. Let's explore this a bit further with this plant in a bottle experiment.

YOU WILL NEED:

- ✔ An adult helper
- ✔ A large (2 liter) plastic bottle
- ✔ Scissors
- ✔ 3 cups of potting soil
- ✔ Plant seeds
- ✔ Cotton fabric
- ✔ A metal skewer
- ✔ Water
- ✔ A trowel
- ✔ A ruler
- ✔ Plant food
- ✔ A pen

1 On the cotton fabric, draw two 1-in (2.5-cm) x 5-in (12-cm) strips, and cut them out.

2 Ask an adult to make three holes at the top of the plastic bottle with the metal skewer, as shown.

3 Cut the plastic bottle in half.

WARNING! SHARP EDGES!

4 Turn the top half of the bottle over and thread the two pieces of cotton through the neck of the bottle so they poke out of the bottom.

5 Then add about 3 cups of potting soil.

6 Scatter seeds into the soil.

7 Add water and plant food to the bottom half of the bottle.

8 Stand the top half of the bottle in the bottom half so that the fabric dips into the water.

9 Give the seeds a little water from the top, and then wait a few days to see what happens!

HOW DOES IT WORK?

Your plant has a supply of water at the base of the bottle, which is carried up the fabric strips into the soil. The moisture builds up in the lower half of the bottle so there's a constant supply of water for the plant. Techies are looking at ways of growing plants in space that are self-contained in a similar way.

Glossary

ACID
A chemical that produces charged hydrogen molecules when dissolved in water.

AIRFOIL
Curved shape used for airplane wings and propeller blades that boosts lift (the force that helps to hold an airplane up).

AIR PRESSURE
The pressure produced by air pressing against a surface.

AIR RESISTANCE
The force that hinders an object's movement through air; also called drag.

ANTENNA
A wire, rod, or other device that transmits or receives radio waves.

ATMOSPHERIC PRESSURE
The pressure produced by the weight of a planet's atmosphere pressing down on a surface.

ATOM
The smallest part of a substance that can be identified as a chemical element.

BACTERIA
Tiny, single-celled living organisms.

CARBON
An element that is a key component of the chemicals that make up living things. When pure, it can exist in several forms including graphite and diamond.

CARBON DIOXIDE
A gas made up of carbon and oxygen.

CASEIN
A type of protein found in milk.

CHEMICAL REACTION
A process by which chemicals combine or change, involving transferring or sharing electrons.

COMBUSTION
The process of burning something.

COMPOUND
A molecule made from two or more elements (chemicals that cannot be broken down into other chemicals).

CURRENT (ELECTRIC)
A flow of electricity.

DYE
A natural or synthetic substance used to change the color of something.

ELECTRON
A tiny part of an atom, carrying a small, negative electric charge.

ELECTRIC MOTOR
A machine that turns electrical energy into motion.

ELECTROMAGNETIC FORCE
The force that operates between electrically charged particles.

ENGINE
A powered mechanism used to transform energy and movement from one type or direction to another.

EVAPORATE
The process of a liquid changing to a gas as it heats up.

FULCRUM
The pivoting point of a lever.

GLIDER
A plane that has no engine but uses its shape to make use of air currents to stay up and to fly.

GRAVITY
The force that pulls objects toward each other. Gravity holds the moon near the earth and makes objects fall toward Earth's center.

HULL
The main body of a ship, most of which is under water.

HYDROGEN
The simplest and lightest element. Combined with oxygen it forms water.

IMPLANTS
Objects that are put into the body, usually for a medical purpose (to replace an organ, for instance).

INERT GAS
A gas, such as helium or argon, from the group of gases known as inert or noble gases. They are stable and don't react with other substances easily.

LACTIC ACID
A naturally occurring acid that is produced in muscles as they work (exercise), and by bacteria in milk.

LAWS OF MOTION (NEWTON'S)
Three laws that define motion: (1) that an object will remain still or move a straight line unless an external force is exerted to move it or change its direction; (2) that force equals mass of an object times its acceleration; and (3) that every action (force) produces an equal and opposite reaction.

LEVER
A device for reducing the effort needed to move a heavy object. Instead of exerting a large force over a short distance, a lever allows the use of a smaller force over a larger distance.

LIFT
The force that holds an aircraft in the air. It's generated in part by the aircraft's wings.

MAGNETIC COMPASS
A navigation device that has a magnetic needle that points to the north.

MAGNETIC FIELD
The field (area in space) around a magnet where its magnetic force operates.

MATTER
Any substance that takes up space—whether solid, liquid, or gas.

MEMBRANE
A very thin sheet or layer that often forms a boundary around a structure.

MICROCHIP
A tiny component of computers and other electronic devices that has microscopic electrical circuits printed on a chip of a semiconductor, often made of silicon.

MINERAL
A naturally occurring chemical compound, usually of crystal form and not a living material. It has one specific chemical composition.

MOLECULE
Two or more atoms joined by a chemical bond. A molecule can contain atoms of the same element or different elements.

MOTOR
A machine that uses a power source, such as electricity or a fuel, to generate movement in a vehicle or other equipment.

NUTRIENT
A chemical that a living thing needs for nourishment, either to provide energy or to build its body.

NYLON
A plastic that is often made into fibers that resembles silk. It is very strong.

ORE
A type of rock that contains metals that can be extracted.

OXYGEN
An element (and gas) essential to life and which makes up about one-fifth of the atmosphere on Earth.

PHYSICIST
An expert in physics, which is the study of movement, matter, energy, and forces.

PIGMENT
A substance that gives something a color or changes something's color when added to it.

PISTON
A rod or plunger that moves up and down inside an airtight cylinder. For instance, there are pistons inside a car engine.

POLYESTER
A synthetic polymer that forms the basis of nearly a fifth of all plastics. Most commonly used as a thread or fabric.

PROPELLER
A set of two or more turning blades, shaped as airfoils, that rotate to move a vehicle through gas or liquid, usually air or water.

PROTEIN
A type of chemical that carries out many different functions in living things. Proteins are considered the building blocks of life.

PROTON
A tiny, positively charged particle inside an atom.

PUMP
A mechanism for moving a liquid or gas from one place to another, either against gravity or more quickly than it would flow on its own.

RADIATION
A type of energy that is released as electromagnetic waves or as tiny particles. It's often used in X-rays. Lots of exposure to it can lead to cancer.

REASONING (AS IN ROBOT AI)
The process of working out a solution to a problem by applying logic to existing information.

RESIN
A sticky substance—like a natural glue—that can be either naturally occurring (produced by some plants) or synthetic.

ROTORS
Rotating parts in a machine.

SATELLITE
An object that orbits a larger body, held in place by gravity. Artificial satellites in orbit around Earth are used for many purposes, including communications and monitoring the weather.

SEMICONDUCTOR
A material that can let electricity pass through it to a limited degree.

SHADOOF
A device consisting of a bucket on the end of a pole that is used to scoop water from a river or pool to irrigate crops. The pole acts as a lever with a central fulcrum and has a counterweight on the end opposite the bucket.

SOLAR (POWER)
Energy generated by the sun's energy.

SPACE PROBE
A robotic space vehicle with no crew that is sent to investigate an area of space (or a planet, moon, or other body).

SPECIES
A group of living things with very similar characteristics.

STEAM
A mist of water droplets produced when hot, invisible water vapor (gas) cools.

STETHOSCOPE
An instrument used to listen to sounds from the body. It has two ear pieces connected by tubing to a small resonator that is placed against the body to pick up sounds.

STREAMLINED
Designed in a smooth shape to reduce resistance when moving through air or water.

TURBINES
Drums with rotating blades inside that are used to produce energy, such as electrical power.

UREA
A waste product made by the body that is usually carried to the kidneys by the blood and excreted in urine.

VALVE
A device used to control the flow of a liquid or gas by opening or closing some kind of flap. It usually allows flow in only one direction.

WELDING
The joining together of material, particularly metal, by compressing after heating.

X-RAY
A type of electromagnetic radiation commonly used in medicine to look inside the body. It can pass through tissue but is absorbed by bone.

ANSWERS

Pp. 18–19 Fantastic Plastic
Puzzle Zone:
Which materials would you use for...
1. Metal—it's stronger.
2. Plastic—it's safer and bouncier.
3. Plastic—it won't lose heat so fast.

Pp. 40–41 Mighty Microbes
Puzzle Zone:
Find the gene code
Brown eyes

Pp. 52–53 Let's Get Digital
Puzzle Zone:
Can you crack the digital code?
The filled in squares form a square shape = return to base!

Pp. 64–65 Restless Robots
Puzzle Zone:
Robot rivalry
1. Robot—the fastest robots can run faster than the fastest human.
2. Human—although by 2017 robots could make pancakes.
3. Robot—some humans can't solve the puzzle.
4. Robot—they can pick faster and they don't get tired.
5. Human—artificial intelligence programs can write poetry but it's not very good.
6. Robot—they're faster and they don't need to breathe air.
7. Robot—some robots are good at this.
8. Human—although robots have been taught to perform magic they don't do as well as human magicians.
9. Robot—some robots do this in factories. And they never lose their tempers when things go wrong!
10. Human—robots aren't known for their sense of humor!

Pp. 66–67 Meet My Robot!
Puzzle Zone:
Robot training challenge

Pp. 72–73 Project Space Station
Puzzle Zone:
Airlock quiz
b) There is no key because there is no lock. There aren't any space burglars to worry about!

INDEX

Index entries in bold refer to experiments and projects